home
astrology

home

paul wade

astrology

creating the perfect home for your star sign

hamlyn

Dedication

To Carol who was with me
To Mollie who was behind me
And to Sarah and Rachel who guided me through.

First published in Great Britain in 2004 by
Hamlyn, a division of Octopus Publishing Group Ltd
2–4 Heron Quays, London E14 4JP

Distributed in the United States and Canada by
Sterling Publishing Co., Inc.
387 Park Avenue South, New York, NY 10016-8810

ISBN 0 600 61092 6
EAN 9780600610922

A CIP catalogue record for this book is available
from the British Library

Printed and bound in China

10 9 8 7 6 5 4 3 2 1

This book combines two subjects that are very popular in the lives of many people today. Interior decoration is a major interest, with countless magazines, books and shows all attempting to make obvious to you how it should be done. More and more people are also realizing the wisdom of investing in their home environment. The design advice on offer ranges from the practical, through the inspirational, to the outlandish.

Unsurprisingly, many still lack the confidence to put such suggestions into practice. Apart from the odd decorative acknowledgement of current trends, most people continue to live in a fairly conventional way. Often, rather than a fear of trying new things or of experimenting with their living space, it's more a matter of coming to grips with all the contradictory material available. With the plethora of advice that is constantly being given, it is hard to know which of these fabulous decorative schemes would really be best for you.

The role of astrology

This is where astrology enters the picture. Astrology is a method for understanding people's tastes, preferences and predilections, and has been around for many thousands of years. Exactly how long is unclear, since such observations easily pre-date existing records, but it is a social and cultural phenomenon which has found its way into many diverse traditions over the past millennia.

Nonetheless just by knowing your date of birth, it is still possible to make some coherent and often surprisingly accurate comments regarding your aesthetic sensibilities and your decorative tastes at home. As the Sun moves predictably through the 12 zodiac constellations every year, we can easily define set periods during which each constellation is particularly emphasized.

BELOW **Understanding the characteristics of your birth sign and the wants and needs of others can be invaluable in the promotion of good social interaction, emotional wellbeing and aesthetic consensus.**

Although this doesn't exclude other constellations from exerting an influence at the same time, it does give us a great start in planning your ideal astrological home. From this point you can then further investigate astrological design for living as you wish.

Astrology's success depends upon a natural inclination for people to try to understand themselves and each other better, striving for a balanced coexistence in harmony with the world. In modern society, it is easy to feel alienated and alone, so it is also vastly preferable to feel part of an instantly recognizable tribal group. You can enjoy a richer and a more widely shared experience and an immediate affinity with people you don't really know. Also, of course, there are those easily accessible guidelines for the better running of your whole life.

Obviously, in order to construct your ideal domestic environment on a fully astrological basis, you would need your complete astrological birthchart and have a pretty good idea of how to synthesize everything from an interpretative perspective. In practice, it would probably be easier to commission the services of an astrological professional, and most probably the advice of a design consultant too, since to find somebody proficient in both skills could prove to be a difficult undertaking.

How this book works

You will find one clearly demarcated scheme for all 12 signs of the zodiac, including all of the following aspects:

- **Typical characteristics** of the sign, together with the factors and priorities that will be important to those born under its influence.
- **Ideal home** of the sign, including immediate impressions on entering the home, general domestic atmosphere and the sign's attitude towards home and family life overall.
- **Relevant element** – whether the sign is associated with fire, air, earth or water, and how this influences taste.
- **Specific design recommendations** for all the main rooms in the house – the entrance, living areas, kitchen, bedroom, bathroom and an extra room that in ideal circumstances you would love to have – including choice of fabrics, wallpaper, art, ornaments, flowers, plants, flooring, window treatments, lighting and special items such as books, chimneys, computers, fountains and jewellery.
- **Combinations with other signs** – in practice one of the most challenging aspects of modern living involves the close proximity of others. To conclude each sign's section, you'll find a few suggestions to help you in sharing your life with members of your own sign as well as others. These describe the strengths of each connection, the difficulties and complexities which you may face together and a guide to harmonious living from a design perspective.

BELOW An understanding of astrological principles can assist you in choosing the correct colour scheme for harmonious living and in planning the right decorative scheme for your home.

how your horoscope influences your taste

The real study of astrology is actually a vast and more than comprehensive subject. Out of necessity, this book can only touch the surface. Any study based purely on your birth sign cannot always account for every factor when it comes to determining your taste and domestic preferences. This chapter looks at the differences between the detailed application of this subject and its more popular presentation, explaining why in certain circumstances things may vary considerably from the outcome anticipated. Such an overview should prove intriguing and serve to stimulate your interest for further investigation.

In order to draw a truly accurate picture of your character and taste preferences, a professional astrologer would need to know three things:

1 Your date of birth. This means not just the day and month but also the year, since the outer planets vary their position on a cycle reckoned over several decades.

2 Your time of birth. Every zodiac constellation rises over the eastern horizon during the course of each day, and the precise time of birth helps to determine the whole orientation of your chart.

3 Where you were born. Because the world comprises many different time zones, the local time in one location is not necessarily equivalent to the local time in another.

Individual birthchart

Having determined this information, the astrologer is able to calculate your own individual birthchart, showing the relationships and interactions between the planets and the constellations for the moment and location of your birth.

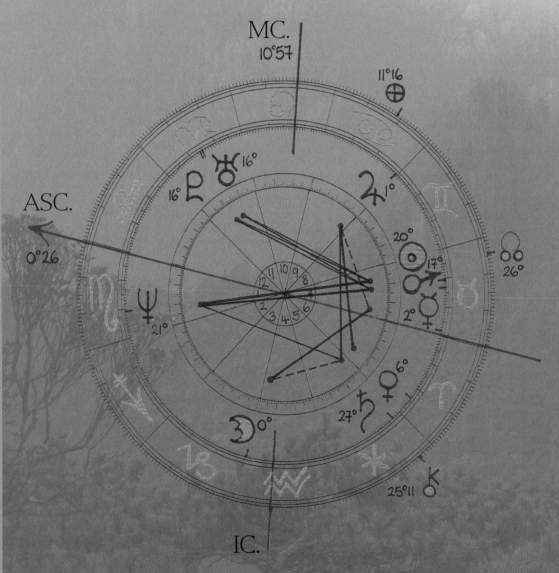

In order to make completely accurate forecasts and predictions which will certainly apply, this really is an essential requirement. It would not be far wrong to consider your birthchart as being unique to you, since two people would have to be born on the same date, at the same location and during the same minute for two charts to turn out to be completely alike. Even with twins there are always important differences.

Signs of the zodiac

Assessing individual birthcharts is not really feasible, however, for more general, popular astrology. Therefore, the division of the world's population into the familiar 12 Sun signs, based on date of birth, acts as a useful guideline, even though in reality it is far from the complete picture. As the Earth orbits the Sun, the Sun appears to pass through each of the zodiac constellations within one year. Its transit of each sign lasts for about a month and the dates are fairly easy to determine (see below).

Western astrology was first developed in the northern hemisphere, where the ingress of the Sun into the constellation of Aries marks the vernal equinox, an annual event otherwise known as the first day of spring. For those more familiar with natural cycles than with any man-made calendar, it was clearly apparent that the planetary year began at this juncture. The lengthening days have reached the same duration as the shortening nights and nature's abundance is renewed after the apparent dormancy of winter. This is why the zodiac traditionally begins with Aries.

Sun sign dates

symbol	sign	dates
♈	Aries	20 March – 19 April
♉	Taurus	20 April – 20 May
♊	Gemini	21 May – 20 June
♋	Cancer	21 June – 22 July
♌	Leo	23 July – 22 August
♍	Virgo	23 August – 22 September
♎	Libra	23 September – 22 October
♏	Scorpio	23 October – 21 November
♐	Sagittarius	22 November – 21 December
♑	Capricorn	22 December – 19 January
♒	Aquarius	20 January – 18 February
♓	Pisces	19 February – 19 March

While the Sun is indeed an important factor in any horoscope interpretation, a great deal more can be determined by looking at surrounding circumstances.

The Sun is the largest celestial body in the solar system, and is very important for an understanding of the birthchart. Astrologically speaking, the Sun is indicative of your fundamental character, of the traits with which you consciously identify, and of how you essentially go about being yourself. It therefore plays a major role in determining your approach to your domestic situation, and indeed to life in general. Your Sun sign is indicative to a large degree of your tastes and expectations, your preferences, likes and dislikes. It is the single most important factor in determining your design choices.

Personal variations

In reality, however, assessing everybody on their Sun sign alone is a little like classifying people on the basis of their nationality. You could say for example that all Scorpios are secretive, all Geminis are madly social and that all Aries people are courageous. This is not really so different from believing that all French people are romantic, all English people are reserved and that all Australians like drinking beer. Indeed such observations may largely be true, yet still within this framework there is scope for some considerable diversity.

Consequently, while this book serves to illustrate the main design criteria for each Sun sign, don't be surprised to find a number of personal variations. Venus, for example, has a great deal to do with matters of taste and can modify the impact of the Sun sign considerably. While always found nearby, it can also be up to two signs away. For example, the Sun in Virgo could mean that Venus is in Virgo as well, but Venus could equally be found in Cancer, Leo, Libra or Scorpio instead. In such instances, although the Sun remains the dominant influence, its impact will be more than a little modified by this additional dynamic.

Other influential factors

Finally, there are other factors contributing just as fully to a complete picture, such as the three qualities and the 12 astrological houses (see boxes opposite for details). Of the latter, the Fourth House has a particular bearing on matters connected with your home and family situation. The Fifth House equates to creativity and often has a special connection with aesthetic appreciation. Then there are other planetary interactions, such as aspects – caused by geometric relationships between the planets at the time of your birth – which will serve to modify this picture even more.

The three qualities

The 12 zodiac signs are divided into four elements, with each element containing three members. The three members of each element are then categorized further according to quality. One sign is termed cardinal, one fixed and one mutable. Each quality therefore contains one sign from each element.

Quality	Signs	Description
Cardinal	Aries, Cancer, Libra, Capricorn	Renowned as the initiators of the zodiac, the cardinal signs are typically active and enterprising. They are noted for their leadership ability, although this can prove surprisingly subtle in its manifestation.
Fixed	Taurus, Leo, Scorpio, Aquarius	Known as the organizers of the zodiac, the fixed signs are generally stubborn, stable, steadfast and intense, with good executive skills and a marked resistance to uninvited change.
Mutable	Gemini, Virgo, Sagittarius, Pisces	Famous as the communicators of the zodiac, the mutable signs are versatile, flexible and adaptable, with a talent for networking and for spreading the word.

The 12 astrological houses

First House   **Indicative of your appearance,** your outer personality, the ways in which you interact with your external environment and the first impression which others form of you.

Second House   **Shows your financial affairs,** your earning ability and attitudes towards the material world in general. Such characteristics accurately reflect your own core values and the things that make you feel secure.

Third House   **Governs communication,** your rational mind, logic and intellect. Rules speech and writing, education at an essential level, your local community and short journeys closer to home.

Fourth House   **Relates to your deepest emotional needs and to your home,** family and private life. Your parents and the impact of the maternal influence are especially detailed here.

Fifth House   **Rules romance,** recreation, holidays, fun, children, pets and sport. Shows creativity and the things you do purely for pleasure. Rules risk, speculation and gambling.

Sixth House   **Indicates your health,** your work and your attitude towards helping others. Also shows your day-to-day routines, your duties and regular responsibilities.

Seventh House   **The house of marriage,** partnership and of all close relationships on a one-to-one basis. Consequently, this also encompasses competitors, adversaries and enemies.

Eighth House   **Indicates shared financial interests,** together with the values and resources of others. More deeply, this house governs birth, death and transformation on every level. It is the house of sex and of life's more profound mysteries.

Ninth House   **This house illustrates your essential religious and philosophical beliefs.** It is linked with further and higher education, freedom, expanded experience and extended travel.

Tenth House   **Linked with career affairs,** with your aims, ambitions and vocation in life. The objectives you aspire towards, the need for recognition and the impact of the paternal influence are also demonstrated.

Eleventh House   **Shows your friends,** what you hope to attain on a personal level and the groups to which you choose to belong.

Twelfth House   **Governs the subconscious mind,** those personal characteristics of which you may be unaware, your dreams and intuition. This house rules seclusion, escapism and psychic phenomena in general.

astrology and colour

Astrology and colour are strongly connected. The astrological tradition has long associated specific colours with particular zodiac signs. At first, these associations can seem somewhat random, but they become more comprehensible once you learn how astrology groups the 12 zodiac signs into the four distinct elements of fire, earth, air and water. These groupings are based on the personality characteristics shared by the three signs within each one. Once you appreciate this, it will be easier to keep the colour associations for each sign in mind. Then, by appreciating how the four elements can blend harmoniously, it will be possible to start suggesting some elemental mixtures of your own.

It has long been appreciated that colour has a marked influence on your feelings and sensibilities. Most people know the difference between waking up to leaden grey skies on a regular basis and to blue skies every day. Those who live in the world's more temperate regions will be familiar with the ways in which the changing seasons and their associated colour schemes can all influence emotional and psychological wellbeing. Think about the differing moods and feelings that are naturally engendered by the subdued watercolours of winter, the rich and vibrant hues of autumn, the shimmering verdancy of spring and the bleached browns and yellows of high summer.

Colour rules

Once you understand the impact that colour can have, it is not difficult to begin indulging in a little colour therapy within your own immediate environment. Simple rules are fairly easy to apply. Reds, for example, tend to warm you up, and blues will usually cool you down. Certain greens can help you to relax, while white confers a sense of space and a clarity of mind. Purples suggest opulence and quality, and yellow a more cheerful and informal approach. Certain shades of light will make you look more attractive, while others are not so flattering.

Although colour is all around you, within your home its proper use is fundamental. The correct use of colour can make the difference between a nurturing and peaceful home environment and one where you will always be feeling stressed, edgy and anxious. Most people already have certain colour preferences, but in terms of astrology there are also particular colours linked to your zodiac sign. Whether or not these have been a part of your preferred

palette in the past, their judicious use around the home will help create your own perfect colour environment. Ultimately, you will feel strengthened and supported within yourself, more comfortable and at peace with the world.

Using an expanded colour palette

Obviously there will be occasions where a choice of more than one colour proves necessary. Some signs are lucky enough to have a range from which to choose; otherwise, through understanding the ways in which astrology's four elements interact, it is possible to select an expanded colour scheme. This will function harmoniously from both an aesthetic and an esoteric perspective.

It's not too difficult to understand which other colours might be appropriate for you. The astrological elements are fire, earth, air and water and each has three signs under its rulership. The signs which comprise each element generally get on well with one another. Fire mixes well with air, since air helps fire to burn and fire helps air to circulate. Earth and water are also complementary, since water makes the earth productive and earth gives water some essential boundaries.

Therefore, in making the correct colour choices for your home, you can also choose additional colours from the same element, or from an element compatible with your own.

Common characteristics

Members of the fire signs are all active, enthusiastic, positive and assertive individuals who will approach life with a keen sense of enjoyment and an enviable vigour. They are not easily deterred or discouraged and will energetically strive to make an impact on the world around them. As they endeavour to put products of their own imagination into practice, they will manifest their own sense of creativity in reality.

Associated colours

The fire signs are associated with variations on the colours of fire in nature.

Aries is perhaps the most central to this range, and covers all shades of red. Crimson, brick red, vermilion, blood red, pillar-box red and scarlet are all under its rulership.

Leo is connected with sunlight colours, so is especially linked with amber, burnt orange, gold, orange, tangerine and darker yellows, for example.

Sagittarius is ruled by Jupiter, and so moves towards a range of more opulent colours, beginning to encompass elements of blue. Indigo, maroon, purple and violet are all associated with this sign.

Combining with other elements

In the real world it's not always possible to live in our ideal domestic setting or to mix solely with those from our own element. Although this is arguably the perfect situation for many signs, a little diversity can definitely have a broadening impact, providing that you're aware of the possible pitfalls and of the shared criteria on which to build.

Earth

Although there is an affinity between certain earth colours and those of fire, members of the fire element should be careful that they do not move too far into the earthy spectrum, where they might experience a deadening effect.

Air

There are important connections between the colours of fire and those of air. This can have important connotations when it comes to living together harmoniously. Although the fire signs associate most happily with one another, they will benefit from extra input involving the air element, and can bring elements of air into their chosen colour scheme. Gemini belongs to the air element, and is linked with paler shades of yellow. Libra is also air, and governs most shades of blue, picking up from the where the deeper tones of Sagittarius end. The elements governed by fire and air are compatible since, without air, fire soon ceases to burn.

Water

Fire and water do not generally make a good mix. Fire's straightforward approach and natural enthusiasm is ultimately extinguished by too much watery sensitivity. The ethereal nature of the water element is easily overwhelmed by the more bombastic fire. The use of rich blues, maroon, indigo and purple is fortunately one decorative avenue where aesthetic compromise can be achieved.

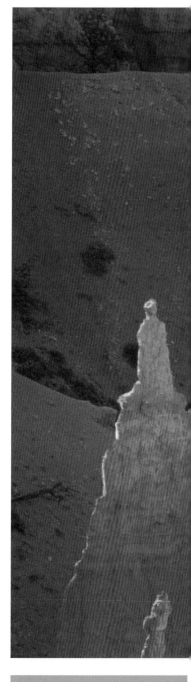

The three fire signs

Aries ♈

Leo ♌

Sagittarius ♐

ABOVE Startling landscapes remind us of the important role that fire has played in the Earth's turbulent past. An inherent affinity is often apparent between the colours of earth and fire.

LEFT The fire signs are associated with all shades of red, from scarlet and bright red through to crimson and vermillion. Within the correct context the effect of reds can be striking.

the earth signs

Common characteristics

Members of these signs all demonstrate a practical outlook and are cautious and methodical in their approach to life. They are generally conservative in their perspective, and are subdued and understated in their tastes and preferences. They have a high regard for durability, for material worth and prefer quality, permanence and workmanship in both their possessions and surroundings. The earth signs don't tend towards impulsive decisions, but will work slowly and carefully towards their goals.

Associated colours

The best colours for members of the earth element are those reflecting the physical reality of nature. Taurus has the broadest range, since Venus, its ruling planet, has a special connection with beauty and with colour in all its forms. Taurus encompasses most pastel tones, with a preference for pale blue, pink and pale green, the main constituent colours of many flowers and natural settings. There are obviously references here also to the colours of fire, air and water, thus showing the necessary harmonious coexistence of all four within an environmental idyll.

   Virgo and Capricorn move further into the spectrum of colours with which the earth element is linked. Virgo governs more muted blues, greens and yellows. It is especially connected with duller, neutral shades such as grey, fawn and mushroom, and is also associated with brown. Capricorn takes the analogy still further. One of the zodiac's most dignified, reserved and conservative signs, Capricorn is traditionally linked with dark brown, dark green, dark grey and black.

Combining with other elements

Members of the earth element are inherently most compatible with their own sign or with other earth signs. However, all kinds of combinations can occur. In each instance it's important to seek common ground where decorative decisions need to be made.

Fire and air

There are connections between the earth colours and those of air and fire in particular. The browns of earth blend into the burnt orange of fire, particularly in semi-desert regions. In turn, Capricorn's black eventually lightens to become the electric blue of Aquarius.

Water

The best match for the earth signs outside of their own element is with signs drawn from the water trio. Earth can benefit from water's influence since, without water, the staid nature of earth becomes infertile and unproductive. It will therefore not cause any harm for watery colours to be gradually introduced into an earthy scheme.

The three earth signs

Taurus ♉

Virgo ♍

Capricorn ♑

ABOVE The browns and dark greens of woodland are characteristic of earthy hues.

LEFT Natural wood is warm, soothing and calming for those born under earth's influence.

the air signs

Common characteristics

These signs display a relatively cool and rational approach to life. Except in extreme circumstances, they are not usually given to huge displays of emotion. The air signs are mentally active, often social and frequently good communicators. They will make design decisions based on logic and from an essentially cerebral perspective. They are especially fond of all kinds of intellectual activity.

Associated colours

Since air is transparent, the air signs are most closely linked with the colours of the sky. Most medium shades of blue are associated with Libra. Dark blues go to Sagittarius and pale blue to Taurus, but almost everything in between is governed by this sign. Libra's connection to Taurus is underlined by its association with pink, together with pale and light green. Both Taurus and Libra are still ruled by Venus, thus accounting for this similarity.

Electric blue belongs to Aquarius, reflecting the startling nature of this sign. The colour associations of air are extended by Aquarius, a sign also connected with turquoise and then with black. Imagine the changing colours witnessed by astronauts as they pass through the outer limits of the Earth's atmosphere, subsequently entering the darkness of space – that's Aquarius. Gemini continues the theme of the sky, ruling pale yellow, the colour of the Sun.

Combining with other elements

Air signs are great together, since they have similar tastes and love to chat and communicate. However, their rational approach and cool emotional response can be enlivened by the input of other elements.

Fire

Air can be enlivened by the presence of fire, since fire's warmth will help the air to circulate. Fire and air are therefore regarded as a good combination.

Earth and water

Earth and water are not good matches for the air element. Despite the colour links from Libra to Taurus and from Aquarius to Capricorn, in the longer term air people will experience too much earth as boring and stultifying. Although there can be air and water affinities based on the individual horoscope, generally speaking this isn't a recommended combination either.

The three air signs

Gemini ♊

Libra ♎

Aquarius ♒

ABOVE Nature often demonstrates the combination of apparently contrasting elements in just the right proportions. Here fire, earth, air and water combine perfectly to produce outstanding results.

LEFT Plenty of light and space is essential for those born under the air element. Many will choose the elevated aspect, stunning views and urban environment of this city loft conversion.

Common characteristics

The water signs are linked together by the strength of their emotional response. They have an active inner life, possess excellent intuition and are extremely sensitive. They are reflective like water itself and can absorb both unpleasant atmospheres and the troubles and the fears of others. All water signs will occasionally need space and time in seclusion to recharge their own emotional reserves. The water signs share a notably spiritual outlook and are renowned for their almost psychic perceptions.

Associated colours

The colours associated with water are mostly the colours of the sea, with all except the palest, darkest and most muted shades of green each proving particularly apt. A major exception is Scorpio, whose former links with Mars have lead to a connection with deep reds, maroon and brown. It is curious, though, that when considering the marine theme many seaweeds are either red or brown, and are scientifically classified according to this distinction. The remainder of seaweeds are of course green.

Pisces picks up where Scorpio ends, with rulership of lilac and mauve, as well as the more obviously appropriate aquamarine and sea green. Finally, Cancer encompasses those shades of green that remain, together with certain blues and white for the foam on the ocean's wave. Silvery and smoky colours also come under Cancer's influence, from this sign's rulership by the Moon.

Combining with other elements

Whilst water with water and water with earth are the classic combinations, there are some possibilities for water and air combinations or even water and fire. However a happy and mutually satisfactory medium will be harder to attain.

Fire

Fire and water don't really mix. The bridge between them is Scorpio, linking in with deep, dark red and brown. Perhaps by following a Scorpio colour scheme, a satisfactory balance could be achieved.

Earth

Water combines well with earth, since earth serves to contain the rather diffuse and amorphous watery nature and to give it structure and form. The colours associated with the earth palette can therefore safely be introduced, as Scorpio's connection with brown may already have intimated.

Air

While there is an apparent tonal harmony between the greens of water and the blues of air, an overly stark and airy theme cannot be deemed suitable for the much more malleable, sensitive and reclusive watery individual.

The three water signs

Cancer ♋

Scorpio ♏

Pisces ♓

ABOVE The beach provides the interface between the earth and the sea. The sea brings its bounty to earth's shores and the earth provides water with much-needed defining boundaries.

LEFT The bathroom is for many water signs the most relaxing room in the house. A bath is preferred to a shower, since contact with the watery surroundings is more prolonged.

♓ ♌

♏

♎

♉ ♑

the zodiac signs

Each sign has a set of natural affinities, and is associated with various modes of

expression, styles, colours, materials and textures. In this chapter you will find the

perfect approach to home design for your own sign, as well as all the others. It will

provide you with all the colourful inspiration and expert guidance you need in

order to create your perfect home environment. Within each individual horoscope

there will always be subtle variations, so don't be afraid to view the following as

suggestions only, to be modified in the light of your own preferences and desires.

Priorities: *action, initiative, self-assertion, speed, being first.*

The typical Aries

Aries is the first constellation of the western zodiac, symbolized by the Ram and coincident with the first day of spring in the northern hemisphere. Its planetary ruler is Mars, and it is traditionally associated with new beginnings and physiologically with the head. In terms of character, those born under this sign are dynamic, active, enthusiastic, positive, courageous, impulsive and brave. They are literally headstrong and love to be the first in many areas, spontaneously leaping in where others fear to tread. Aries subjects don't take kindly to limitations or restrictions and usually favour activities in which there is plenty of scope for action and physical energy. This sign is generous and willing to be of assistance, yet is often described as selfish and egotistical.

The Aries home

Aries folk love to keep busy, so their homes always prove a hive of activity. Yet interior decoration and the beautification of their domestic surroundings may not, in practice, be as high on their list of priorities as they might wish. Even where other astrological influences alter this situation, there is always so much else to be done, so many places to go and so many people to see that the home situation easily moves downwards in the list of overall life goals. The average Aries is great at beginning things, but not always so persistent when it comes to pursuing matters through to a successful conclusion. While favourably disposed towards ambitious renovation, decoration and home improvement projects, their interest soon wanes once the initial challenge is past. Thus in the average Aries home a conscious effort should be made. It will be important to avoid a demoralizing descent into domestic chaos.

A fire sign

Aries is a fire sign and favours action, initiative and energy. The home environment should allow plenty of space for movement and activity. From time to time, the habit of beginning things and then abandoning them halfway through can lead to a depressing build-up of unfinished projects, the remnants of which it will ultimately become necessary to address. It is

Characteristics

Favourable

Pioneering • enterprising • adventurous • brave • direct • enthusiastic • active • autonomous

Less favourable

Impatient • impulsive • aggressive • egotistical • inconsiderate • selfish • temper • rash

Sign associations

Symbol The Ram

Ruling planet Mars

Day of the week Tuesday

Lucky colours All shades of red

Lucky number Nine

Birthstones Ruby and garnet

Metals Iron and steel

Flowers Aloes, cacti, chillies, garlic, geraniums, ginger, holly and honeysuckle

Trees All thorn-bearing trees and shrubs

Regions England, Germany, Israel, Lithuania, Palestine, Poland and Syria

Cities Birmingham (UK), Florence, Krakow, Leicester, Marseilles, Naples and Utrecht

Best partners Leo, Libra, Sagittarius and often Capricorn

Worst partners Cancer

Ten key factors

east
fireplaces
flaming and discordant hues
hardware
metal
red
roofs
spices
tools

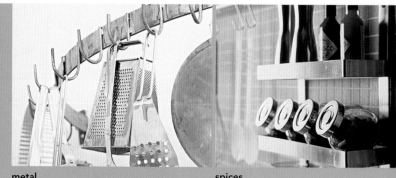

metal   spices

therefore vital to make the time for such regular sessions of clearing and organization. Although spending time tidying may seem boring, it will guard against the cramped and restricted feeling which will otherwise ensue. This can be far more detrimental in the longer term.

Having a good clear-out in the home has a positive and therapeutic impact, with a certain joy experienced in the action of removing the old.

ABOVE The typical Aries will feel at home in a space with clean lines and modern features. Splashes of red are toned down with areas of white and wooden floorboards provide continuity.

red   fireplaces   hardware

Making an entrance

In practice, the entrance to the Aries home can easily acquire a rather neglected air, since you are always too busy either rushing in or out to give the necessary thought to its appearance. However, in ideal circumstances a front door of sturdy construction would be best, to withstand the inevitable rough treatment that you will inflict in terms of loud bangs and slams, as well as bumps and scrapes from carrying large and unlikely objects inside and outside. Traditional wood is probably the most suitable material, rather than alternatives such as glass which might more easily become damaged.

   The ideal colour for the Aries front door would be a bold, bright red. A shiny, gloss finish is far more appropriate for your exuberant character than a more muted look. Almost any shade of red would suit, but generally speaking the louder the better. A brass knocker and fittings help complete the dashing impression.

Living areas

Aries subjects are renowned for beginning projects and then losing interest halfway through. Both sexes have a propensity for DIY. Many possess a love for tools and an interest in the intricacies of assorted household machinery. Either way, once your unfinished projects start to build up, the potential for mess is considerable.

   Consequently, the Aries living area is best organized from the perspective of space. Clean angular lines and an absence of clutter will get matters off to a promising start. The colour red needs to be used sparingly indoors, but can feature as a matt finish for large areas of flat colour such as walls, either when wallpapered first or just painted directly. Colour can then be graduated from dark to light to give a feeling of depth and space and the judicious use of white helps protect against possible overkill.

   Since Aries is a fire sign, it would be ideal for real flames to feature somewhere too. This could be anything from a traditional wrought-iron fireplace, in an older property, through to the high-tech metal and glass construction of a modern wood-burning stove.

Flooring

Ease of cleaning and maintenance will be the key here, so laminates, linoleum, resin or even painted floorboards are all a good idea for you. Ceramic tiles would work well too, possibly in terracotta, white or a light, plain colour. Decorative rugs in bright colours could be used throughout, with carpeting where required in neutral, plain colours only.

Lighting

Lighting in your home will be recessed and modern. There will be no strip lights or fluorescents, with spotlights and modern wall lights instead. Daylight will generally be plentiful, with painted shutters, roller-blinds and Venetian blinds replacing more troublesome and old-fashioned curtains.

ABOVE A sturdy, bright red front door is very appropriate for an Aries home. A brass knocker, door handle and letter box complete this bold statement.

Fabrics and wallpaper

Fabrics with a smoother texture, such as silk, are recommended for you, along with those that are plainer and more functional, such as cotton and linen. Heavy and embossed patterns are not suited to an Aries environment and will conflict with the feeling of space and simplicity that you like to maintain. Sheepskin is particularly linked with the sign of the Ram, and man-made fleeces are an excellent modern equivalent.

Kitchen

Classically, Aries eats to live instead of the other way around. Consequently, the kitchen is unlikely to be the busiest room of your house, with sporadic bursts of activity around mealtimes rather than a steady stream throughout the day. An extensive selection of labour-saving appliances proves essential, since you have far better things to do than the washing-up. A dishwasher is therefore a vital item on the agenda, along with a microwave, chest freezer and a good supply of frozen ready-meals.

Since, traditionally, the sign of Aries has a particular link with iron, steel and metal in general, the extensive use of stainless steel in the kitchen is likely to hold a special appeal. For larger areas such as the sink, draining-board, cooker, splashback and work surfaces, it would work best with a brushed finish, to avoid a somewhat overwhelming shine.

The use of cooking spices also comes under the rulership of Aries, so some carefully selected spice jars will make a good addition. These could be stored on glass or metal shelves and, with a clean, modern appearance, would complement the overall picture very well. In terms of seating, a breakfast bar is the perfect choice, with shiny chrome stools for the brief perching of hurried visitors.

ABOVE The perfect Aries kitchen is clean and modern with a stainless steel cooker and tiled floor. A breakfast bar is ideal as it fits in with the active Aries lifestyle.

Bedroom

As the first sign of the western zodiac and with physiological rulership of the head, Aries is also linked with the top of the house, with chimneys and with the roof. In a dwelling with more than one storey, it is recommended for you to sleep upstairs, and an attic conversion would probably prove ideal. Even where this option does not exist, the ability to sleep well above the ground is particularly suited to this sign. Younger or more athletic Aries subjects might enjoy a gallery bed – a raised platform reached via a ladder, which would also appeal to their pioneering spirit. Others might simply favour a higher than usual base to the bed, with space underneath for storage of clothes.

Cupboard space will be essential in your bedroom, so that there is at least the possibility of organizing your possessions. A hatstand would prove a useful addition, since this sign often favours headgear. The sparing use of red in the bedroom will promote a degree of passion, but a largely darker ambience will encourage peaceful repose.

ABOVE As Aries like to sleep well above the ground, a dynamic raised bed like this one is ideal. It also provides useful storage space for tidying away clutter.

Bathroom

Aries is not a sign that spends hours in the bathroom, since inevitably there is always so much more for you to do. Showers will be preferred to baths for their expediency, with powered razors and toothbrushes for much the same reason. However, a good long soak can serve to relax the over-stressed Aries subject after the travails of the day. A few drops of relaxing aromatherapy oil can serve to assist this process, with candlelight promoting both a restful response and emphasizing the fire element to which you belong.

A tiled finish in the bathroom area will be easy to keep clean, for both walls and floor. The frequent use of pink in bathroom ceramics is unlikely to appeal to you as a substitute for red, so it might be better to aim for a largely white look overall, with dashes of spot colour to continue with this colouring theme. So long as light levels are sufficient, cacti and aloe vera are two Aries plants that would thrive in a bathroom environment. An unusual wooden carving or piece of metalwork would help provide a focus for the eye.

Art and ornaments

Aries is associated with sharp cutting tools, woodcarving, metalwork and welding. A few choice woodcarvings or one or two metallic sculptures would prove ideal for you. The favoured metal for Aries is iron, so any wrought ironwork would be a great addition, but nowadays steel can definitely be considered to be a suitable substitute.

Flowers and plants

Thorn-bearing plants come under the rulership of Aries, as do all spiky and prickly specimens. Cacti and succulents, which are native to hot and dry locations, also express the Aries principle very well. Almost any variety of cactus, aloe, agave, or sansevieria can be used around your home, with the angular nature of their habit serving to complement and enhance the stark, modern lines featured in such an interior. Imaginative but minimalist planting can be used to good effect, especially in conjunction with stones or gravel.

ABOVE The Aries bathroom should be clutter free and easy to keep clean. A striking specimen plant such as this dracaena serves to accentuate its angular lines and contemporary feel.

Extra room

With the interest that many Aries subjects express in the use of tools and in the intricacies of different types of household machinery, your special room would ideally comprise an area away from the rest of the house where you can indulge your hobbies fully. For male Aries, this might well be fulfilled by the traditional garden shed, where you can set up your vice and workbench and spend a calming hour or so away from the distractions of everyday life. You would enjoy servicing household and garden machines, since this sign has a special association with engines and with engineering. Tinkering with things that are broken, trying to repair them and get them working again will always stimulate your desire for a challenge. Should a garden shed not really be a viable option, a few hours of car maintenance would exert a similar effect, in a covered garage, carport or outside. Of course, such activities are not exclusively a male preserve.

A more conventionally feminine approach might involve practising a few favoured arts and crafts. A room inside the house where such activities could take place unhindered would therefore be ideal for you – somewhere where the clearing-up does not always need to be done immediately.

ABOVE Despite the exuberant and sociable nature of Aries subjects, you also like to have somewhere to hide away and indulge your hobbies unhindered.

Combining with others

Other Aries

Lots of energy here and, providing that you both keep busy together, everything should be fine. Difficult issues might include who makes the design choices and who gets left to finish things off, but the energy of your ruling planet Mars is well expressed through DIY activities.

Taurus

Taurus may prove too traditional in their choices and a little too hard to get motivated. Nonetheless, crossover aspects between Venus and Mercury can lead to some very similar design decisions, with your courage to initiate matters followed through with Taurean staying power.

Gemini

A complementary match. Aries appreciates the breadth, scope and sheer quantity of Gemini's design ideas. Gemini is happy that someone is so receptive to these and willing to try them out in practice. Persistence can be required to ensure that matters are completed fully.

Cancer

Sentimental Cancer is nostalgic, loving antiques, traditional techniques and the past. Dynamic Aries is always pushing forwards, favouring newer designs and cutting-edge materials. Since Aries is good with tools, perhaps helping Cancer to repair some more valued heirlooms might assist in a compromise.

Leo

A good mixture, with both signs going all out for their preferences. Leo won't hesitate to make suggestions and Aries won't hesitate to mention when they disagree, and vice versa. With both signs sharing the same fiery approach, a happy compromise is sure to be achieved.

Virgo

Virgo is too conservative for Aries, and is often fanatically neat and tidy around the house. The Aries habit of leaving uncompleted projects in sundry locations won't be viewed sympathetically. In order for these two to live together happily, they need their own separate spaces.

Libra

Aries and Libra are a good mix. Aries will make all the design decisions, with Libra taking care of the finishing touches and ensuring that everything looks beautiful at the end of the day. Libra can be a little indecisive at times, so will appreciate the positive Aries nature.

Scorpio

A stressful combination. Aries is far too loud and flamboyant for reserved and brooding Scorpio. The Scorpio likes to live in privacy and Aries wants to be noticed all the time. Both signs like red, though, so perhaps they could at least agree on a colour scheme.

Sagittarius

Both of these are active and enthusiastic characters, so some creative sparks are likely to fly once they get together. Aries will encourage Sagittarius to put their ideas into practice. Sagittarius will encourage Aries to broaden their horizons. Both signs love open fires.

Capricorn

Conventionally, these two are not supposed to like each other. However, in practice they often find a lot to admire. Capricorn is impressed by the Aries initiative, with Aries admiring Capricorn's dedication, persistence and staying power. With a little understanding, some great decorative choices can be made.

Aquarius

This is a combination that often works well. Aries likes to be the first with everything and Aquarius is often well ahead of their time. These two can experiment with all the latest décor and materials, as Aries begins new projects and Aquarius follows them through.

Pisces

Rather a difficult mix. The Pisces idea of interior design is far too floaty and ethereal for Aries, who likes everything to be cut and dried with strong and clearly defined lines. All that voile and muslin is likely to prove rather annoying, although you might learn something about relaxation.

taurus

Priorities: *security, stability, comfort, sensuality, material focus.*

The typical Taurus

Taurus belongs to the earth element and to the fixed quality, so in theory you can't get much more stable and rooted. Traditionally, Taurus is seen as solid, dependable and steadfast, with a dominant focus on the material side of life. In recent years, the cosmic machinations have overturned this traditional image somewhat, causing many Taureans to act quite unpredictably and to throw caution to the winds. Traditionally and at heart, though, they still aim for steadiness and reliability – they are fond of their routines, their security and particularly their food. The emphasis on material security is augmented with an emphasis on security of purpose. Certainly anyone wishing to change the mind of the average Taurean could have a very long struggle ahead. In relationships, these people are sensual, tactile, loving and affectionate, but they can also prove extremely jealous and possessive of those that they love. A Taurean's anger is slow to surface, but once roused can be truly terrifying.

The Taurus home

Taureans are often seriously attached to their homes and belongings. They view such factors as a secure and worthwhile investment in an unstable world. With comfort and security such important objectives, the overall experience of the Taurean home will be a relaxing and revitalizing one. The dominant impression is one of peace and safety, of rest and relaxation, of comfort and of deep contentment, with a pleasurably unhurried and timeless feeling permeating throughout.

Older Taureans usually have tastes which were firmly set in earlier life. Taureans of all ages generally veer towards the conservative and the traditional and, as far as financial constraints will permit, towards the plush and the luxurious. A fondness for expensive sofas, monster television sets, king-sized beds, large baths and so on would be typical.

Being ruled by Venus, the aesthetic sensibilities of most Taureans are well developed. Many have a marked interest in architecture and in interior design and will be well aware of the ways in which the potential of their current residence might be developed further.

Characteristics

Favourable

Practical • patient • reliable • persistent • dependable • affectionate • cautious • determined

Less favourable

Possessive • lazy • inflexible • stubborn • resentful • self-indulgent • boring • greedy

Sign associations

Symbol The Bull

Ruling planet Venus

Day of the week Friday

Lucky colours Pale blue, pale green, pink and all pastel shades

Lucky number Six

Birthstones Emerald and jade

Metals Brass, bronze and copper

Flowers Daisies, foxgloves, lilies, poppies, primroses, roses and violets

Trees Apple, ash, cypress, fig and pear

Regions Capri, Cyprus, Greek islands (especially Rhodes), Ireland, Switzerland and Tasmania

Towns and cities Dublin, Eastbourne, Hastings, Leipzig, Lucerne, Palermo and St Louis

Best partners Capricorn, Virgo and Scorpio

Worst partners Aquarius and Leo

Ten key factors

art
beauty
comfort
carpets
food
northeast
pastels
possessions
security
sculpture

food

sculpture

An earth sign

Taurus is a zodiac sign that enjoys a particular focus on the physical and the material sphere. It belongs to the earth element and so will favour an emphasis on the use of natural materials. As a sensual and tactile sign, the use of texture proves an even more important feature. This can effectively be used both to enhance the natural feel and ambience of the Taurean interior and to satisfy that other great Taurean need, the desire for comfort and for luxury. Taureans also make great gardeners and it would be most uncharacteristic if at least one or two plant specimens did not find their way into the house. Lilies are often linked with you, but beware of the pollen stains.

ABOVE White or cream predominates within a sumptuous and cosseted atmosphere. The overstuffed sofa, with soft sheepskin and carpet underfoot, spells pure luxurious indulgence for the Taurean living areas.

carpets

comfort

security

Making an entrance

An emphasis on personal and domestic security is of major concern to Taurean subjects. Being ruled by Venus, however, there is also a strong connection with beauty, design and form. Consequently, you are likely to feel happiest when the entrance to your home is well defended – except where invited guests are concerned, in which case you will make them very welcome.

A solid and secure front door made from traditional oak, or a sustainably produced tropical hardwood, would thus appeal both to your aesthetic sensibilities and to your desire for safety, retreat and sanctuary. As practical souls, you will be delighted about its durability and warmth, the painstaking craftsmanship that has gone into its production and its ability to withstand ever-changing climatic conditions. The wood should be stained a natural colour, to best maintain its essential grain and character. Taureans won't mind paying a little extra for what is considered to be a lasting and worthwhile investment.

Living areas

The living areas of the Taurean home are geared to indulging in unlimited ease and relaxation. Soft furnishings will therefore prove a critical feature. An enormous, over-stuffed sofa, bought mainly for comfort but also for good looks, would make a perfect focal point; it must be one on which you can easily stretch out fully.

Luxurious ageing leather has the bovine provenance especially connected with this sign, but floral patterns would suit older Taureans and would be in keeping with their gardening exploits. Plain white settees and suites would suit the aesthetic sensibilities of the more contemporary-minded.

Older furniture is not discarded but rejuvenated through the use of voluminous throws in luxurious-feeling materials such as satin, velvet and chenille. Taureans are sensual beings and you simply adore soft fabric on your skin. You love the old and familiar and are really sorry to have to get rid of anything. Providing your furniture remains comfortable and welcoming, it is unlikely to be replaced with anything new.

Living areas should be softly carpeted, for walking in slippers, bare feet, or in very little at all. While an open fire would be ideal, in reality central heating would help cut down on unwelcome extra labour.

ABOVE The entrance to a Taurean home should always be secure. Here the ornamental trees and overhanging balcony are certainly attractive, yet still encourage a feeling of protection.

Fabrics and wallpaper

The sensuality of Taurus lends itself well to fabrics that feel good as well as looking good. Thus satin, velvet and silk are excellent choices, with floral prints favoured by older Taureans to remind them of their love of nature. Likewise, you may be drawn towards textured wall coverings such as flock wallpaper. In practice, however, you could do better by aiming for relative simplicity, using softer textures.

Flooring

Taurus actually rules carpets, which means that it is the zodiac sign most closely associated with this type of floor covering. So carpets are recommended, wherever practicable, through the house. Generally speaking, the deeper the pile and the more luxurious the feel, the better the carpet will suit you. Alternatives include plain floorboards, maximizing the warm feel associated with natural wood, or in certain instances a flooring of natural stone for its permanence. However, the latter would definitely need to be kept warm enough to enable barefoot comfort throughout the year.

Lighting

Used carefully, lighting helps to enhance a feeling of relaxation, and should largely be soft and romantic in character for the Taurean home. Dimmer switches should be fitted throughout to allow the light levels to be adjusted to fit your prevailing mood. Decorative light fittings in bronze or brass are especially suitable for wall lighting. Otherwise, a fairly traditional outlook prevails, with floor-standing or standard lamps used to good effect and table lamps with fabric shades to match the prevailing décor of the room.

Kitchen

Since Taureans love food, the kitchen receives great emphasis within your home. As a sign, Taureans divide into two camps where food is concerned: the ultra-conservative and the gourmet. The former prefers a strictly limited menu, with no use of spices or unfamiliar ingredients. The latter embraces wholeheartedly a far more exotic taste experience. In terms of personal development, for fun and as a worthwhile hobby, Taureans should always try joining the gourmet camp.

ABOVE A traditional approach predominates in the Taurean kitchen. Earthy colours feature and the use of a traditional butler's sink with a stylish complementary swan neck tap works well.

Taurus rules trees in general, so most kitchen features should be made of a richly coloured wood. Stone, clay or quarry tiles are your favoured flooring. Should your budget and circumstances permit, a range-type cooker would be the perfect complement to this idyllic picture, ensuring the year-round warmth, comfort and security that are so vital for your emotional wellbeing. Such a feature epitomizes the permanence, solidity and traditional values that are so accentuated in Taurus.

As a finishing touch, a good strong bookshelf could be lined with a varied collection of the latest culinary tomes. A few bottles of red wine, port and perhaps brandy help matters to proceed with a swing.

Bedroom

Taurus is ruled by Venus, famous as the planet of love, but Venus is also associated with comfort, luxury and sensual pleasures of all kinds. Taureans are certainly capable of hard work, but you also place relaxation high on your agenda. The pleasures of restful sleep will be notable for you. In the Taurean bedroom, there will be a great emphasis on physical comfort and sensual pleasure. Expect a huge bed with a soft mattress, a voluminous quilt of the finest down, additional cushions covered in sensual fabrics such as satin or velvet and numerous large pillows. There will be a radio and a portable television for those extended Sunday mornings in bed and a luxurious shag-pile carpet on the floor. You will also pay considerable attention to additional decorative features, such as lamps and light fittings, to complete this sumptuous picture.

Typical colours for the Taurean bedroom include pinks and lilacs. Taureans of a more traditional persuasion might incline towards the more frilly and fussy. Male Taureans left to their own devices will maintain a more utilitarian approach.

Art and ornaments

Taurus is linked with alabaster, architecture, all forms of art, brass, bronze, copper and sculpture. Hence art and sculpture are likely to feature prominently within your ideal home, with paintings or bronzes especially favoured. Taurus loves quality and you will probably view art as a worthwhile investment, so a few large key pieces would be better than more numerous but less splendid alternatives. Some decorative fixtures and fittings in brass or bronze are recommended too.

RIGHT The female Taurean is often very feminine. Male Taureans favour a less fussy approach, but here no detail has been omitted to render life at its most comfortable.

Bathroom

Your bathroom can also provide plentiful opportunity for physical delight. The bath itself will be an important centrepiece, since you are much more likely to bathe lengthily than to take a quick and functional shower. The bath will be huge and perhaps of an unusual design. A circular bath would suit modern homes and an ornamental roll-top bath would be great for more traditional ones. A few drops of rose oil added to this would be perfect for creating the right ambience.

Taureans especially like a carpeted bathroom, since you adore comfort underfoot and loathe colder alternatives such as tiles or vinyl. However, cork or plain wooden flooring provides a practical alternative, with mats and rugs scattered round for extra comfort where necessary.

A heated towel rail will be essential, with a collection of huge, thick towels very much in evidence. Plenty of shelf space will be necessary for all the cosmetics, creams, powders and so forth that are essential for the Taurean ablutions. A thick bathrobe in an equally plush material hangs ready on the back of the door.

ABOVE The Taurean love of luxury inclines you towards a carpeted bathroom. However, an equal fondness for quality and permanence could render warm flagstones a more practical alternative.

Flowers and plants

As an earth sign, Taureans are often particularly fond of plants and flowers. Easy access to the outdoors is ideal, perhaps a set of French windows, a balcony or even windowboxes where space is at a premium. Ideal Taurean plants include scented roses and lilies for cut flowers, or violets and gerberas for a splash of colour to grow as potplants indoors.

Extra room

With the Taurean fondness for food and the association of Taurus with the gourmet, and bearing in mind the need for material security common to all members of this sign, the ideal extra room for you would be an old-fashioned larder. Of course, this may not be practicable in every residence and would probably suit a rural rather than more urban existence, but for a sheer reflection of Taurean priorities such an addition would be hard to beat.

Walk-in larders are traditionally dark and windowless, with a stone floor to maintain a temperature lower than that of the external environment. Here you could store and keep all the exotic ingredients essential for your next epicurean adventure, but which may only be used once in a while and would otherwise clutter up the kitchen shelves. With such an arrangement, you could also buy huge cheeses, hams and salamis and store them perfectly. Fine wines could be purchased by the case and would await enjoyment when the time is right. On a more prosaic level, the security-conscious Taurus will be happy to know that, should disaster strike, you will always be ready with enough to eat.

BELOW Taureans are famous for enjoying their food. You'd find an old-fashioned larder a wonderful addition to your home, ensuring you never ran short of enough good things to eat.

Combining with others

Aries
Aries is too forceful for Taurus and not concerned enough with comfort around the home. They are always changing things, too, just when you had grown used to how they were. Although this combination does work under certain circumstances, it is definitely not the easiest.

Other Taurus
Physical comfort is certainly going to be a major feature when these two get together. Without doubt, it will be overstuffed sofas, shag-pile carpets and huge fluffy towels all the way, with kitchen cupboards groaning beneath the weight of luxury foods.

Gemini
You are going to need to make some compromises. As a Taurean, you like life to be ordered and to progress in a methodical manner. Gemini is too mercurial for you, but does have a good logical mind, so always talking things through will help with planning your home.

Cancer
Taurus and Cancer are great together, and nowhere is this more obvious than in the kitchen. Cancer loves to cook and you love to eat, so what better combination is there? You are both traditional in your tastes and both want your home to be as comfortable as possible.

Leo
Both Taurus and Leo are fixed signs, which means you can be quite obstinate once you have made up your mind. Some diplomacy may be necessary when it comes to matters of taste and décor, with personal comfort proving a promising area for finding common ground.

Virgo
Both signs have a strong grounding in reality and concern for the material world, so you will both be fond of good furniture and of quality materials used to construct your home. It will be when your are budgeting for further improvements that you can really appreciate one another's financial abilities.

Libra
You are both ruled by Venus, the planet which most closely governs interior décor and design in general. Thus there is a strong sense of a shared aesthetic here. Although you may differ with regard to its exact application, it can be a great guiding principle.

Scorpio
You are opposite in the zodiac, but not opposite in your views. You actually have a great deal in common. Taurus aims to build a luxurious nest in which Scorpio will be happy to hide away. Although you may differ over colour schemes, you are essentially a complementary match.

Sagittarius
Sagittarians will want to fill their home with sundry pieces of unusual and ethnic art. They like weird sculptures they have gathered while travelling all over the world. You are far more staid and traditional, so some potential for disagreement should certainly be noted.

Capricorn
Capricorns like to present a good front to the world. They will always strive to make quality purchases, an attitude with which Taurus can sympathize perfectly. Although Capricorn's tastes are at times a little austere, a largely happy relationship will usually result.

Aquarius
Aquarius is the most progressive sign and yours is one of the most traditional. You find it hard to appreciate how somebody can disregard conventions which have served so well for so long. Trouble is likely unless you can allow one another a great deal of space.

Pisces
When it comes to home design, Taurus and Pisces mix rather well. Taurus can concentrate on the bigger elements, the structure of the room itself and the larger items of furniture. Pisces enjoys the finishing touches, such as smaller areas of colour and imaginative window treatments. A complementary match.

Priorities: *communication, thought, learning, variety, sociability.*

The typical Gemini

The constellation of Gemini is named after the Heavenly Twins and is symbolized by its two brightest stars, named Castor and Pollux. Communication is the primary focus for Gemini subjects. This sign enjoys talking, writing letters, socializing, chatting on the telephone, sending and receiving e-mail. Its subjects like to be busy, have an inherent curiosity and are always learning. They are often active in their local community, running around their neighbourhoods in a constant quest for knowledge and intellectual stimulation. They simply loathe sitting about doing nothing and if forced to do so will become anxious, fretful and bored. Geminis are versatile, adaptable, articulate, clever and have a great deal of nervous energy. Their main failing is a possible lack of focus, so they should strive to keep their agile minds occupied for greatest success. This sign is ruled astrologically by the planet Mercury, so it is no coincidence that this planet is frequently chosen as a symbol for telecom companies and newspapers worldwide.

The Gemini home

Geminis are extremely sociable and just love being out and about in their local community, talking with people and enjoying the latest buzz around town. Parties and other gatherings are definitely the spice of life for this sign. Gemini is much more closely associated with towns and cities than with the countryside, and could never contemplate living an isolated existence. Much of their time indoors is spent talking on the telephone, reading, writing letters, sending and receiving e-mail or otherwise keeping contact with a wide and diverse range of friends and acquaintances. Visitors to the home – including family, friends, work contacts and neighbours – are often numerous.

Without such social interaction, the average Gemini would find matters unbearable, and would be left with moving the furniture around to break the monotony. Consequently, many times when you visit a Gemini home, you will find that everything has been rearranged. This helps the Gemini to pass the time, and also engenders a sense of variety within the home environment, which in turn stops the ever threatening onset of boredom.

Characteristics

Favourable

Versatile • adaptable • lively • intelligent • communicative • spontaneous • witty • busy

Less favourable

Anxious • nervous • superficial • unsettled • cunning • irresolute • scattered • inconsistent

Sign associations

Symbol The Heavenly Twins

Ruling planet Mercury

Day of the week Wednesday

Lucky colours Yellow, especially the paler shades

Lucky number Five

Birthstones Agate, striped stones generally and topaz

Metals Mercury

Flowers Ferns, lavender and lily of the valley

Trees All kinds of nut trees

Regions Belgium, Iceland, Morocco, Sardinia, Tunisia and Wales

Cities Cardiff, London, Melbourne, Nuremberg, Plymouth, San Francisco and Tripoli

Best partners Aquarius, Libra and Sagittarius

Worst partners Pisces, Scorpio and Virgo

Ten key factors

books
broadcasting
cars
communication
duality
hallways
letters
magazines
posters
streets

books

communication

An air sign

Geminis are sociable, communicative and mentally active. Your home should be light and well ventilated, with plenty of daylight and lots of fresh air. It should be uncluttered, although your busy life and activities away from home can sometimes lead to unresolved issues of organization. There is always a spare room, sofa bed or mattress available for those staying over, and extra crockery, cutlery, wine glasses and usually alcohol to assist with social interaction. Even a Gemini needs some peace and quiet at times. On these occasions nothing is more favoured than curling up with a good book or an interesting magazine.

ABOVE **The Gemini living area has plenty of visual variety, space and light. It is focused around a central coffee table, where friends can perch to chat.**

magazines

duality

letters

Making an entrance

Gemini subjects don't like to stay in much. Here, however, there is a definite disparity between male and female members of this sign, with female Geminis often typifying the social butterfly to a far greater degree than the more introverted male. Nonetheless, neither sex would wish to do without external stimulation for very long. The perfect Gemini front door would therefore either be made of glass, or would have big windows nearby to minimize the separation from the outside world. You would generally prefer to live on a busy street rather than behind hedges or at the end of a driveway. To continually be aware of what is happening in your immediate surroundings closely approaches your ideal.

Nearly any cheerful bright colour would be good for the exterior paintwork, although paler yellows do have a particular association with this sign. Aside from this, Geminis are youthful in their outlook and always like to keep abreast of the latest happenings in fashion and design. Consequently, there will be certain fashionable touches as you enter your home, with more than a nod towards the latest design trends.

ABOVE The Gemini front door incorporates plenty of glass, either in its design or in its surrounds. Those at home will always want to see what's happening outside.

RIGHT The Gemini kitchen is cheerful and chaotic, with plenty of useful ingredients and utensils on open display, where they can easily be reached.

Living areas

The ideal Gemini living space is simple, uncluttered and easy to keep clean, while still maintaining plenty of features to catch the attention and to prove interesting for the eye. The basic structure of your living area should therefore be quite simple, with fairly neutral colours for the walls and with a plain floor, perhaps of polished wood. By staining the wooden floor a darker colour than the walls, a lighter, more airy and more spacious feel will be engendered.

Ideal Gemini furniture is probably typified by a clean and modern design. Curved lines are most suitable, since you are always rushing about and are likely to bruise yourself on any angular corners. A multicoloured feel would help to stimulate your attention, with pastel shades more suited to such a context than bright, primary colours. Different items of furniture with a cohesive overall feel help to maintain greater interest than strictly matching suites, sofas and chairs.

Geminis like to perch, so stools and other items of seating intended for a short stay suit your lifestyle better than large armchairs. The focal point must be a large coffee table, with plenty of additional seating for visitors.

Flooring

Tiles are great for Gemini wherever possible, because of their utility and their easy-care nature. Mosaic tiles in interesting patterns are fantastic, with rugs and wooden slatted duckboards for wetter locations. Wooden floors are best suited to your living areas. These could either be left plain and varnished, stained an interesting and natural colour, or painted with special floor paint.

Lighting

Lighting in your home will be streamlined and modern. Gemini subjects hate harsh overhead lighting, so avoid strip lights and fluorescent lighting wherever possible. Bars of adjustable halogen spotlights are chosen for kitchen areas, with angled spotlights for desks and other corners. 'Daylight' bulbs are useful for you in winter, but you prefer natural daylight. Large windows are perfect for such airy individuals.

Kitchen

Geminis will not spend a great deal of time in this room. You will mainly be rushing in to grab a cup of coffee or a bowl of cereal on the way out, or will be enjoying a chat with some friends you have invited over to share a meal. Consequently, a utilitarian approach is most likely to work, with an uncluttered feel that is easy to keep clean. Simply stripping and then painting the floorboards is a beautiful yet functional idea in such a situation. Adequate storage is also crucial, with wall racks for hanging some brightly coloured cups. Either glass- or open-fronted cupboards will be very useful for storage, and could be used to display some richly coloured crockery. Drawstring bags

Fabrics and wallpaper

Gemini is most closely associated with cotton. While almost any colour could find a place in the great scheme of things, you definitely have a preference for more natural fabrics that can breathe, an important priority where all air signs are concerned. Comfort and quality are factors, too, with areas of pattern and decoration forming attractive highlights for your soft furnishings. Otherwise, wallpapers should be plain, and painted walls would probably provide a more satisfactory solution.

LEFT The Gemini bedroom needs adequate built-in wardrobe space, to keep your belongings clutter free from the outset. Otherwise where will you store all those clothes, shoes, toiletries and other fashion accessories?

Art and ornaments

Gemini generally favours modern art, and you would like a few colourful pictures or prints gracing primary locations in your living space. Although personal taste is a factor here, this sign is traditionally associated with the poster – so anything which could broadly be defined as poster art would be a good choice. Typical ornaments are sleek, modern and long-necked vases, usually in metal or glass. The dual nature of this sign means that you love mirrors, either of the decorative variety or as part of an interesting piece of furniture like a coffee table.

for holding clothes pegs, carrier bags for recycling and other sundries would help to complete this functional picture.

The ideal centre point for your kitchen would be a breakfast bar, with a few high stools or chairs for sitting and chatting. Positioned in front of the sink and cooker, you can then maintain a running conversation while getting on with more mundane tasks. A kitchen television would stop you getting bored if no more stimulating company was present.

Bedroom

You are likely to view the bedroom as a fairly functional area; yet, despite your reputation for incessant and frenetic activity, you actually need more sleep than many other signs. To keep life running at the pace this mercurial sign demands is very taxing to both your nerves and your physical resources, so adequate rest and relaxation is particularly important for a sign more predisposed towards burnout than most.

Neutral colours will therefore be best for the walls and pastel colours for the bedroom furnishings, with heavy curtains or shutters to exclude the light. Any unwanted sensory stimulation, or intimation that a new day has begun, is likely to get your mind on the go again and will correspondingly render sleep less likely. A bedside table, bedside lamp and a good book are essential additions which would certainly help you to unwind. Otherwise the general environment should be unfussy, with a minimalist yet welcoming atmosphere prevailing, which enables you to switch off once your busy day has ended.

Bathroom

The Gemini bathroom should follow the same clean, clear and airy lines that will characterize the remainder of your residence. A tiled finish throughout will be both practical and beautiful, with the intricate nature of mosaic tiles perfectly suited to the fondness for detail which characterizes this sign.

Mosaics could be in one colour, differing shades of complementary hues, or largely in plain white with highlights of spot colour. Interesting effects can be achieved with an iridescent finish or by using a reflective tiling medium such as glass. Should colour predominate on the walls, floors and ceiling of the bathroom, then plain white for the bath, sink and other fittings is almost certainly best.

Lighting in the bathroom should be unobtrusive, perhaps with recessed halogen wall or ceiling lights. A well-lit mirror will be essential both for personal grooming and for increasing the feeling of light and space. Any sources of natural light should not be obscured with curtains or blinds, but can be made opaque with a frosted, patterned or sandblasted effect. This will ensure your privacy while maximizing light input.

Flowers and plants

Ferns and lily-of-the-valley are traditionally associated with Gemini and members of this sign often have a fondness for other lily varieties too. However, you are typically not the best at regular care or watering, since you are often either not at home or easily distracted by other, more pressing concerns. Thus growing plants is not a good idea for Geminis and cut flowers will soon lose their sparkle. Artificial flowers are therefore perfect for you. There are some amazingly realistic specimens now available to those who choose carefully.

Extra room

With the focus on communication so characteristic of this sign, the ideal extra room for a Gemini would have to be a study. Here you could keep all your books, your surplus magazines and all the torn-out pages, photographs, cards and other indispensable items which you undoubtedly believe could find a useful application one day in the future.

Geminis have many friends with whom they need to keep in touch. It is likely that nowadays these friends will be dotted in assorted locations around the world. Thus a desk for writing, with drawers for envelopes, stamps, writing utensils and writing paper will be a notable focal point. There will be a conventional telephone, although most likely of the cordless variety, which can be carried easily around the room and won't stop you from doing other things simply because you are currently enjoying an extended conversation. There will be a charger for that most typically Gemini of all items – the mobile phone – as well as a fax machine and a long-suffering computer with which to send and receive e-mail and to surf the worldwide web. This will be a late and recent model, but unfortunately will often be found creaking under the weight of inadequate care and maintenance.

ABOVE Gemini is a communicator and is always writing letters, making telephone calls and sending e-mail. A dedicated study is the ideal location for keeping everything in one place.

Combining with others

Aries
A happy mix. Gemini likes the sign of Aries, since its members are always ready to try anything and won't hang around once they have decided to do so. Aries also favours clear lines and design principles, thus assisting the Gemini's escape from a sea of clutter.

Taurus
You will find that, in reaching a decorative compromise with Taurus, a number of your own principles have to be abandoned. You are very flexible and they are very obstinate, so often you will acquiesce for the sake of peace. Of course, this isn't really the best basis for a long-term association.

Other Gemini
You are both so mercurial that, while there will always be plenty of variety within your home, it could be hard to find a scheme with which to stick for very long. Also, you are always out and are easily distracted, so the plans you do have might never be fully implemented anyway.

Cancer
You have a tendency to neglect your home and are usually out. You probably think of Cancer's tastes as rather dull. Nonetheless, it is good that they are so focused on the domestic situation, because you will really appreciate this care when you come home.

Leo
Similar colours are associated with both your signs, with yellow for Gemini and orange for Leo. Besides, you both share a number of creative ideas. You are certainly intrigued by Leo's outrageous taste, so long as you can get to use some of your own concepts occasionally.

Virgo
Gemini finds Virgo rather dull. Earthy colours, minimalist schemes and coarse fibres have you loudly yawning from the start. You simply long for the odd detail, for a little interest and intrigue. Since Virgo hates your untidy ways, this definitely isn't an ideal match.

Libra
Gemini and Libra are both air signs. You will love the easy-going Libran approach and their profound appreciation of the aesthetic. In turn, your lively mind and versatility will encourage the Libran to consider new concepts. A good design match.

Scorpio
Gemini is sociable and loves a house full of people. Scorpio is private and can't think of anything worse. Scorpio is possessive and likes to know where everything is. Gemini scatters their possessions about randomly. It is not impossible for these two to live together – the question is, should they?

Sagittarius
Geminis quite like the informal Sagittarian style. It is relaxed and easy-going, with a lived-in atmosphere and plenty of space. Unfortunately, Sagittarius prefers the countryside and Gemini is more of a city dweller, but otherwise they are a good mix.

Capricorn
Capricorn's tastes are steeped in tradition, while Gemini likes to try many different things and maybe not to stick with any of them for long. Capricorn believes in a strict set of design rules whereas Gemini is far more eclectic in their taste. This isn't really a perfect match.

Aquarius
Gemini is easily bored and needs lots of variety and interest. Aquarius rules change, so life could not be dull with them around. Aquarius exerts a stabilizing influence on Gemini, helping them to discuss and to pursue their ideas in a more concrete form. These two can go far.

Pisces
Although Gemini and Pisces are both mutable, they have a very different decorative approach. Pisces is a little too ethereal for your tastes, finding seclusion very important and often liking to keep the curtains drawn. You, by contrast, are very social and love fresh air.

Priorities: *home, domesticity, nurturing, family, the past.*

The typical Cancer

Cancer is a complex sign. It is most easily understood by thinking of the animal which this constellation represents. The Crab is hard on the outside, with a strong outer shell, from beneath which the world is cautiously surveyed. The Crab hides behind fearsome claws and approaches life from a sideways trajectory, but underneath is one of the softest, most gentle and most caring signs of all. Ruled by the Moon, Cancerians are particularly prone to the fluctuations of this celestial body. One minute they are moody, withdrawn and unapproachable, the next a kinder and gentler person you could not hope to meet. Above all, the most important issue for a Cancerian is their home. Belonging to a warm, caring and nurturing domestic and family environment is of major importance to their physical and emotional wellbeing. In particular a strong maternal relationship is always of lasting importance. This may not always be easy, but is always powerful and will always exert a major and lasting impact.

The Cancer home

Cancer is ruled by the Moon. Of the whole zodiac, it is the sign most closely associated with domesticity, with the home and with family life in general. Thus the ideal Cancerian home will also be home to a large family, with many relatives and their assorted friends generally making themselves comfortable whenever they happen to be visiting, passing or are otherwise feeling the need. The atmosphere of the perfect Cancerian home will be rather chaotic, but every resident and visitor is individually welcomed, recognized, fed and is made to feel uniquely supported in their own individual needs.

There is an undeniable and all-pervading atmosphere of safety, warmth and homely bustle about the Cancerian home. This is not the tidiest of signs and hates to throw anything away, so neatness and organization will never be primary features. Yet what may be lacking in terms of structure and order will be more than balanced by such liberal helpings of gentleness, thoughtfulness and emotional warmth. Think about the ideal family home as just perfect for the average Cancerian. You won't be far wrong.

Characteristics

Favourable

Protective • nurturing • parental • kind • sympathetic • tenacious • thrifty • shrewd

Less favourable

Hypersensitive • over-emotional • unforgiving • cowardly • touchy • snappy • moody • crabby

Sign associations

Symbol The Crab

Ruling planet The Moon

Day of the week Monday

Lucky colours White, silver, smoky grey, silvery blue and green

Lucky numbers Two and seven

Birthstones Moonstone and pearl

Metal Silver

Flowers All white flowers – white roses, acanthus, convolvulus, lilies and water lilies

Trees Maple, and other trees that are rich in sap

Regions The Netherlands, New Zealand, Paraguay, Scotland and USA

Cities Amsterdam, Manchester, Milan, New York, Stockholm, Tokyo, Venice and York

Best partners Pisces and Scorpio, possibly Capricorn

Worst partners Aries and Libra, possibly Capricorn

Ten key factors

antiques
cooking
domestic life
families
food
gardens
glass
north
nostalgia
water

cooking

glass

A water sign

Cancer is best described as sensitive, emotional, intuitive and very deep. All members of the water element regard their homes as a sanctuary, a place to escape from the harder edges of the outside world and to safely recharge their emotional and spiritual resources. The perfect Cancerian home will reflect these qualities of withdrawal, of containment and of emotional security. It may be almost womb-like in the sense of complete enfoldment. Comfort is naturally an important factor in such circumstances, as is a link with the past. Being particularly associated with collectables and antiques, the typical Cancerian would very much like one or two family heirlooms on display.

ABOVE A warm, nurturing and quite traditional atmosphere is best for the home-loving Cancer. You'll need plenty of comfortable seating for when family members and their friends call round.

gardens

water

families

Making an entrance

Of every room in the house, Cancer is most closely associated with the kitchen. You love matters to be friendly and informal where close friends and family members are concerned. Therefore, it would be ideal for them to enter your home through the back door, immediately illustrating that they are a trusted and regular visitor, someone who already thoroughly knows the ropes. The back door will either be open or they will have been informed of the key's location, perhaps even given one themselves if they have visited a little more than occasionally.

With any luck, they will come straight into the kitchen, because in many circumstances this is where they will be spending the majority of their stay. They will also get to arrive through your fabulous Cancerian garden, which is most probably of the crowded cottage variety. Every plant bursts skywards in an ecstasy of vim, vigour and abundant herbaceous joy.

Living areas

In all probability, the main living area in your ideal Cancerian home will be the kitchen, or at the least will need closely to adjoin this part of the house. Most Cancerians love to cook and enjoy a myriad of other domestic activities, so this area is always going to be one of your most heavily used. In terms of cooking, eating, relaxing and even working, the kitchen probably is going to witness the heaviest use of all. However, everyone from time to time needs to escape from their usual surroundings.

The ideal Cancerian living space will be comfortable rather than smart, with a generally relaxed and lived-in feel, encouraging visitors to kick off their shoes and relax. Cancerians are quite traditional in outlook and often feel a strong connection with the past, so a few older and slightly distressed items of furniture will add to the generally somewhat time-worn feel. A few choice antiques will not go amiss, either, although these will need to make a practical contribution to your domestic environment, not simply to exist as sterile objects to be admired from a distance. A large well-stocked bookcase and a prominent display of family photographs help to complete the homely feel.

Flooring

Flooring in your home will need to be hardwearing and practical, since traffic from assorted family members, visitors and friends is likely to be considerable. Tiles or plain stained and varnished wooden floorboards will be great in more utilitarian areas, with natural fibres and sheepskin in places where more comfort is required. Hardwearing carpet in natural tones would otherwise certainly prove a conventional and a traditional alternative.

Lighting

The ideal Cancerian lighting should be indirect, diffuse, gentle and romantic. Natural daylight is enjoyed and privacy can be maintained with imaginative

ABOVE Cancer is more likely to confer the gift of green fingers than other signs. The Moon's passage through Cancer is often the best lunar influence for planting.

Fabrics and wallpaper

Traditional floral patterns and chintz suit older Cancerians. While making something of a comeback, for a more contemporary feel such fabrics should probably not be overused. Plain walls are the safest choice nowadays, with distressed or weathered paintwork contributing to a comfortable, homely and unpretentious atmosphere. You will almost certainly prefer natural fabrics, with a welcoming touch.

ABOVE A traditional beamed country kitchen is perfect for Cancer. Note the enormous wooden dining table, known to the whole family as the hub of the home.

exterior planting, patterned or stained-glass features and internal drapes made from chiffon, gauze, muslin, organza or voile. Otherwise, your interior lighting is likely to be fairly traditional, although modern design features can help to provide a more contemporary slant. Table lamps and standard lamps will undoubtedly both have their place in the typical Cancerian home.

Kitchen

Here we find the hub of your home. Cancer is perhaps best suited to the typical country kitchen, with the main centrepiece an enormous wooden dining table. Here much of daily life will take place – cooking, eating, coffee, conversation, socializing, dealing with the morning post, telephone calls, sundry work tasks and responsibilities, and children playing.

A medium-coloured wood represents an ideal theme for such a room, with traditional glass-fronted cabinets in which to keep your extensive collection of crockery. Other cooking utensils can be hung from hooks around the walls, with available surfaces covered in a selection of old-fashioned enamel bread bins and other useful containers, ready for the extensive range of cooking ingredients which the average Cancerian is likely to need. Earthenware and terracotta pots, tureens for those special occasions and a pair of manual

cooking scales would be typical items to have dotted about. A few open wall-mounted wooden shelves could provide useful additional storage space.

Finally, terracotta or stone tiles complete the picture underfoot, with some freshly cut flowers rounding off the countryside feel. A few bunches of dried flowers are a useful substitute during winter's darkest days.

Bedroom

The bedroom is your ultimate sanctuary. It is here that your fondness for comfort and the colour white is most likely to show. You will favour a cosy or even luxurious bed, with many extravagant pillows and the best quilt money will allow. A wrought-iron or wooden bedstead would be perfect, with white as the predominant theme for the bedclothes, providing a classic and a timeless feel. Light levels in the bedroom should not be too high, and can be diminished during the daytime with muslin or voile hung in the windows to diffuse glare. Some subtle embroidery around the edges of the bed linen would be a great complementary feature, helping to prevent the overall impression from being too plain.

Otherwise the Cancerian bedroom should be quite simple, although certainly never austere. This is a room for sleeping and for privacy, which

ABOVE Cancer favours white and a clear light, with semi-transparent fabrics used to lessen glare. Here the bedroom exudes a feeling of safety and protection, without appearing claustrophobic or confined.

Art and ornaments

Antiques are particularly associated with Cancer, so a few items of antique furniture would make a perfect addition. Photographs and pictures of your ancestors and of your immediate family are likely to be prominently displayed. An interior water feature is strongly recommended for its relaxing and spiritually uplifting impact. Vases and bowls are also loved by this sign, whose main characteristics emphasize both enclosure and containment.

therefore should not be that busy where additional decoration is concerned. The walls could be hung with a few family pictures, as important reminders of past happy times. As much storage as possible in the form of drawers and cupboards will help prevent your hoarding instincts from cluttering up the place too greatly.

Bathroom

The bathroom is an important room for the Cancerian, the first of the zodiac's water signs. White would be an excellent overall colour, with a few touches of green or blue to break up an excessively stark impression. The use of plain wood for doors, shelves and other features helps encourage a feeling of comfort and of warmth. The introduction of a few carefully chosen natural elements such a pebbles, stones or seashells helps to bring the outside world inside the home.

You will probably prefer baths to showers, although the presence of the latter could provide an excellent opportunity for a little interesting glasswork by way of a shower screen. Otherwise, an old-fashioned cast-iron bath, with the depth in which to luxuriate fully, would probably prove ideal. Finally, some plump white towels, a thick white bathrobe and a heated towel rail will help ensure bathtime remains a sensual and an emotional delight for you.

Flowers and plants

Of all the zodiac signs, Cancer is typically the one with the greenest fingers. Almost all plants will thrive under your influence. Plants themselves are always likely to be a welcome and prominent feature in any Cancerian home. Cut flowers are used for dramatic effect, but the desire to nurture means that mostly those plants that are potted and still growing are favoured. All large white flowers are particularly associated with this sign. White lilies are especially attractive indoors, and are justifiably renowned for their alluring aroma.

LEFT The bathroom is a great opportunity to accentuate your watery theme. Here functional white walls and ceramics highlight found driftwood and a dry sponge from the seashore.

Extra room

With such a focus on the family, on children and on parenthood, the recommended extra room for you would be either a bedroom or a nursery for the children. This would be in constant use when they are small, can be converted to a den as they grow, and later will find further application when the grandchildren are descending for a more than welcome visit.

At the height of its usefulness, this special room should certainly be decorated in a style consistent with the rest of your house. This will probably veer towards the rural and the contemporary, providing a nurturing and comfortable environment in which it would be perfect for the children to grow. Plain wooden beds and other furniture are both warm and practical. They can be varnished to increase durability and can be decorated with interesting stencils and motifs. Cane, rattan or wicker baskets, shelves and other accessories are both sensible and attractive, matching wooden items with similar colours and textures.

Woven jute or coir matting on the floor will enhance these warm natural tones. Sisal is an alternative to these materials, but can be a little coarse. It is usefully combined with generous sheepskins in areas where greater sensitivity is required.

ABOVE Cancerians love children, so a child's bedroom or nursery is the perfect addition. Lavish care on your offspring like no other, but remember when to let go.

Combining with others

Aries

Cancer likes the home to form a protective cocoon. You are fond of the old and familiar and are often nostalgic for the past. Aries views life in broad strokes, often sweeping away one decorative scheme in order to bring on the new. Poor Cancer is soon feeling rather disturbed.

Taurus

Taurus appreciates quality possessions and finds it hard to let go. Cancerians love their home and also cling onto the past. Soon a substantial buffer of furniture and ornamentation builds up around you. It would not appeal to everyone, but for you two it is just great.

Gemini

Cancer is too clingy for Gemini, much too nostalgic and attached to bygone styles and attitudes. Gemini likes to change the furniture around and often never seems really to establish any permanent home base. There should not be any major difficulties between these two, but there probably isn't much affinity either.

Other Cancer

You would imagine that staying at home and thinking about domestic issues would be an ideal pastime for these two. However, with both of you inclined to hoard and to hold onto every memento from your past, it could soon become quite difficult to breathe amid the clutter.

Leo

Cancerians love their home and Leos love children and animals. In a rambling property overrun with such things you could have a lot in common. Leo likes to be the centre of attention and can be insensitive, but otherwise you probably wouldn't mind them showing off too much.

Virgo

Virgo is very practical and is always able to put Cancer's latest decorative ideas into application round the home. The ideal Virgoan design scheme is perhaps a little too minimalist and stark for many Cancerian tastes, with their tidy nature causing certain disagreements over clutter.

Libra

Libra primarily loves beauty and Cancer loves their family, so there could be some cause for conflict when family members start disrupting the carefully planned Libran design scheme. Otherwise there will always be minor tensions between these two signs.

Scorpio

Cancer and Scorpio are both water signs, so are reflective by nature and value seclusion from time to time. Home functions in both instances as a place of sanctuary and withdrawal. With a shared attitude towards nesting such as this, a happy relationship is surely guaranteed.

Sagittarius

Traditionally incompatible, this combination is in practice more common than you would think. Cancer stays at home and provides a settled home base while Sagittarius gallivants around, remaining safe in the knowledge that home is always there. Both signs enjoy a similar flavour of relaxed country-style living.

Capricorn

These two are opposites and the mutual attraction can be strong. Cancer can indulge their decorative and design fantasies, while building a warm and caring family home. Capricorn earns the money to pay for it all, while getting a glow of satisfaction from being such a good provider.

Aquarius

Cancer is nostalgic and loves the past. Aquarius usually will be looking forwards to the future. Paradoxically, though, Aquarians are often also curious about very ancient times. With a little Cancerian care this could blossom into a rewarding shared interest.

Pisces

You are both water signs, so you share similar attitudes and will empathize completely with one another from an emotional perspective. The Cancerian shell makes them rather tougher and better organized, though, so they will help protect Pisces from life's harder knocks.

Priorities: *self-expression, glamour, success, creativity, the best.*

The typical Leo

Leo's symbol is the Lion. As the ruler of the beasts, they demand due homage from those lesser beings who surround them. Their ruling planet is the Sun and their natural position is therefore at the centre of things. However, not all Leos are the flamboyant show-offs so often favoured by astrological literature, many are much quieter yet still able to command a similar degree of attention and respect.

These are truly generous, loyal and big-hearted individuals, never happier than when in a position of authority and prestige. Given the admiration and esteem they feel they deserve, there is nothing that the average Leo wouldn't do for those they love. This sign likes the best of everything and will suffer severely if forced to put up with the mediocre and the second-rate. However, their love of children and animals means that no sacrifice is ever out of the question. Noble is an excellent word to describe them.

The Leo home

Leos like the best of everything. This is a sign associated with royalty, presidents, prime ministers and leaders of all descriptions. In practice, though, not every Leo is born into or can graduate to such exalted circles. In fact, many prefer to rise to the pinnacle of achievement at a far more comfortable position in society, rather than to feel inadequate and overwhelmed in a challenging and less certain situation.

Therefore, while this sign is one especially linked with castles, palaces, impressive ballrooms and with other such illustrious structures, in real life, wherever a Leo finds himself you can be sure that this is their own personal castle too.

The Leonine fondness for children and animals frequently leads to a home environment that is overrun with pets and human offspring, in which case circumstances are unlikely to be as grand as would otherwise be so. A marble hall with statues may be perfect in the Leonine imagination, but in practice a much more humble dwelling filled with adoring subjects will probably prove far too hard to resist.

Characteristics

Favourable

Magnanimous • generous • noble • chivalrous • creative • expansive • wholehearted • dramatic

Less favourable

Pompous • snobbish • conceited • spoilt • obstinate • bombastic • affected • show-off

Sign associations

Symbol The Lion

Ruling planet The Sun

Day of the week Sunday

Lucky colours Sunlight colours – yellow, gold and orange

Lucky number One

Birthstones Diamond and amber

Metal Gold

Flowers Sunflowers, marigolds, celandines, cyclamen, rosemary and passion flowers

Trees All citrus trees – especially orange, bay, olive trees and all palm trees

Regions France, Italy, Macedonia, Madagascar, Romania, Sicily and Zanzibar

Cities Bath, Bristol, Bombay, Chicago, Los Angeles, Madrid, Philadelphia and Rome

Best partners Aries, Sagittarius and in some circumstances Pisces

Worst partners Taurus, Scorpio and often Aquarius

Ten key factors

ballrooms
castles
creativity
children
luxury
palaces
pets
picnics
playrooms
warmth

children   warmth

A fire sign

Leo manifests an active and enthusiastic approach to life. This sign is especially associated with creativity and with the things people do for fun. Consequently Leo is linked with pets and children, since for many childbirth and child-rearing are essentially creative acts. Otherwise, Leonine creativity manifests as an interest in art, drama or the entertainment industries. Yet this term really just implies the ability to bring to concrete manifestation those products of their own imagination, the things they would like to put into practice in their daily lives. To do so takes energy, confidence and zeal. The typical Leo has all of these factors in plentiful measure.

ABOVE Leos love glitter and glamour, so an average or understated living arrangement simply isn't for you. Here the golden fireplace and animal print recliner both speak loudly of your Leonine roots.

pets

picnics

luxury

Making an entrance

No matter where the Leo home is sited, there will be something about its entrance that catches the eye. If circumstances permit, initial impressions will be very grand indeed. Marble steps and pillars, with an imposing and heavy mahogany front door are just a couple of possibilities. The Leo love of gold translates into a huge brass door-knocker and matching brass fittings. The Leonine residence is reached at the end of a long gravel driveway, which passes through avenues of trees. The house rises majestically in the distance for some time before it is actually reached.

In practice, not all Leo houses will be quite so magnificent. However, they will be distinguished by having something bigger and better than those around them. Yours will be the house with most ornate bell, the largest nameplate, the biggest windchimes or the most prominent satellite dish. Alternatively, it is simply the house with all the lights on and the curtains wide open.

Living areas

In theory, you would like to live in a palace. Think marble floors and pillars, statues and fountains, chandeliers, huge windows, balconies and vast staircases. Fitting such expectations in with the average environment is not easy, but as you love quality, you will seek to surround yourself with this wherever you can. You are less worried about the expense and are more concerned with living in a manner befitting both your own expectations and those of your family and friends. You just couldn't stand to feel embarrassed or ashamed when your friends or neighbours come to call.

Bright and contrasting colours can be used with impunity in the contemporary Leo home, because if anyone can both appreciate and carry off such striking tones then it is definitely you. Reds, oranges, yellow and gold are particularly suitable, although you certainly wouldn't need to stop there. With the Leo connection to sunlight, large windows and plenty of natural light are a considerable plus. More flamboyant features such as swags and tails around windows, upholstered pelmets and curtain valances might also find their place. Comfortable sofas and armchairs are essential.

Flooring

The ideal Leo floor will be easy to care for and keep clean. Modern rubber floors come in a variety of colours and feel warm underfoot. Luxurious carpeting also appeals to your sensibilities, and terracotta tiling would certainly be appropriate from a colour perspective. For a real taste of luxury, though, how about an embossed black leather floor? An ultra-modern solution, this could be perfect for you in a well designed bedroom.

Lighting

With Leo's rulership of the Sun, it will be important to maximize the Sun's rays within your home. Large windows and skylights are therefore recommended.

ABOVE Don't anticipate slipping quietly into this home. You'll be greeted with all the genial fanfare and bravado that your arrival richly deserves. Let's hope you're up to the occasion.

Fabrics and wallpaper

Certain fabrics are just made for Leo. Where they would find a place in the scheme of the contemporary Leo home is debatable, but there is usually some scope for their deployment in covering sofas, cushions or windows. One typical Leonine fabric is gold lamé, where gold metallic threads are woven into various fibres. Certain modern metallic sheers produce a similar effect, when linen and acetate yarns are mixed together.

Where maximum exposure is not possible, it is best to compensate with the use of natural and daylight bulbs, especially during times of lowered light intensity. Otherwise sunlight-coloured drapes at the windows can produce a similar effect, making you feel it is sunny even when that isn't actually the case.

Kitchen

The Leo kitchen is likely to be modern and utilitarian. It will be replete with all the latest labour-saving devices, since there are obviously far more important matters demanding your attention than the washing-up and the drying of clothes. This equipment will all have been purchased new and, depending on your individual level of awareness with regard to these things, comprises the latest models of the most respected brands.

All of the fire signs like modern kitchens, and stainless steel would be favoured by Leo. The flooring should be unobtrusive and easy to keep clean; ceramic or rubber tiles are excellent choices, or a polyurethane rubber

ABOVE Leos love to entertain, so when visitors arrive the last thing you'll want to do is disappear off to prepare the meal. This more convivial arrangement is so much better.

flooring that is poured into place. The rubber alternatives enjoy the added advantage of being warm underfoot. Leo, as a Sun worshipper, hates the cold.

A prominent wine rack containing some select choices completes this area, with a few luxury items for when guests come to call. You are probably not the most committed of cooks, but always love to entertain.

Bedroom

The bedroom, as the most private and personal area of the house, is where your love of luxury can most find expression. The centrepiece of the bedroom area is of course the bed itself. A big, bold statement will help to get matters off to an excellent beginning.

It simply wouldn't be proper to consider any low-level bed or modest futon for the Leonine repose. Far more appropriate will be an immense double bed with a mammoth frame. The most outrageous choice of all would be a variant of the traditional four-poster bed. A more modern wrought-iron specimen might prove a less extravagant first choice although, for those who would really like to shine and whose circumstances permit, there is really no substitute for the traditional wooden bed.

At the very least, most Leos will be able to make a straightforward sleeping area into somewhere very special, simply by draping some suitable material over your bed to form a canopy or corona. The shag-pile carpet is also an essential touch where ultimate luxury is concerned.

Bathroom

The Leo bathroom should follow the clean and easy-to-maintain lines that are prevalent in other areas of the house, but should always be warm and welcoming, remembering how all Leos dislike cold. Underfloor heating might therefore be particularly luxurious within such a context. Small mosaics of tiles on the walls – comprising the many colours of sunlight from yellow, through gold to burnt orange and even darker – would create a warmer atmosphere. Bold primary colours could be used to highlight certain features of an otherwise plain bathroom suite and would continue the sunshine theme throughout the room. Venetian blinds maintain your privacy while still allowing maximum daylight to enter your home.

ABOVE In the heart of the lion's den no compromise will prove acceptable. Tastes vary between the traditional and more modern, but will always be as opulent as possible.

Art and ornaments

Leos are often particularly fond of art. A couple of large pictures hung in prominent positions would certainly make a striking focal point. You like your artistic statements to be bold and on display, perhaps where suitable with antique gilt frames to highlight other golden themes. Otherwise, mirrors make ideal ornaments and are great for helping you to catch sight of yourself at regular intervals. The Sun motif could prove a useful theme.

Brass fittings would be good in your bathroom area, bearing in mind the Leonine predilection with the colour of gold. Mirrors should be plentiful, so that you can always be of sure of presenting a suitable face to the world. Lighting should be bright and direct but always flattering. Recessed halogen spotlights, cleverly set into the walls and ceilings, will probably prove most suitable for a Leo bathroom.

Finally, though, don't forget the all-important 'throne' – the toilet. The design must fit in with the rest of the room, but in addition an opulently padded seat might be considered essential. An area of the home that many could forget about, here it provides the ultimate piece of pampering where Leo is concerned.

BELOW This bathroom combines the sunset colours of yellow, orange and black with which your sign is particularly associated. The clever use of brass fixtures and fittings completes this effect.

Extra room

Given sufficient space and the perfect situation, the ideal extra room for a Leo household would have to be a solarium. Members of this sign are ruled by the Sun and are often sun-worshippers in the extreme. During the brief summer months in temperate climes you are often to be found at the beach, or in gardens, parks and other public spaces, soaking up every last drop of that precious UV. To have an indoor facility where you can work on your tan in year-round privacy, ready for those few moments of glory, would surely be your idea of bliss.

If such an area could be expanded to include a sauna, gymnasium or even a swimming pool, so much the better. Leos aren't particularly drawn to exercise, but pride in your appearance will certainly incline you towards the cultivation of a toned physique. Where this simply isn't possible, to have an area to squeeze a horizontal or a vertical sunbed would always be fantastic. Just to feel those rays on your skin will always put you in a much better frame of mind. No matter what your natural colouration, a little sunshine always helps provide a further healthy glow.

Flowers and plants

Leos are not always great with plants, so may prefer the artificial or dried variety to anything alive. Cyclamens are a good Leo houseplant, but should always be watered by standing in water, rather than risking their crown rotting by watering from the top. Another undemanding plant which could prove very suitable for Leo is the gerbera or African Daisy – yielding large and striking flowers in yellow, red, pink or orange in response to only the minimum of care.

LEFT It is a rare Leo indeed who does not love lying in the Sun. Being able to do this whatever the weather and even at night is your ultimate luxury.

Combining with others

Aries
You are both fiery characters, so, when faced with those inevitable disagreements over matters of taste and décor, neither of you will be reticent when it comes to boldly stating your case. Luckily, you probably won't need to disagree that often. Fiery colours suit both of you.

Taurus
You are both fixed signs, so can be very obstinate. You have wildly differing views and, if you are not careful, it could soon develop into a situation involving the immovable object versus the irresistible force. Basically, a fairly loose association is the only solution.

Gemini
Generally a good mixture, since you share a number of similar decorative and design principles. Some compromise will be necessary eventually, or Gemini may grow tired of Leo being right all the time. Leo in turn feels peeved by Gemini's obvious lack of respect.

Cancer
Although at times you will find Cancer's approach a little reserved, understated and traditional, it is great that they are prepared to take a back seat where your own style options are concerned. Also, you will share a mutual interest in children and animals.

Other Leo
Put two Leos together and you will certainly end up with a house that everybody's going to notice. Flamboyant, luxurious and grand will probably be something of an understatement, so you may need to exercise some caution in order that ostentation and pretension don't enter the picture too.

Virgo
Leo likes everything to be bright, grand and larger than life. Virgo likes everything to be minimalist, subdued and understated. You could comprise by using a minimalist approach with only top-quality materials, as long as everyone is aware of the costs involved.

Libra
Libra can be indecisive and is also very partnership focused. Leos are confident, sure of their own correctness and love to be in command. In this association Leo will be making the design decisions and Libra will be mostly happy to go along. Sounds wonderful, doesn't it?

Scorpio
There could be some disagreements here, since Leo wants more than anything to be noticed, and that is the very worst thing so far as Scorpio is concerned. Such a pairing can only work if Leo takes all the attention and praise, while Scorpio can function unnoticed.

Sagittarius
This is a good pairing, since Leo and Sagittarius are both fire signs, thus sharing similar attitudes and a similar perspective on colour and design. Relaxed country-style living will suit them both. When Sagittarius disagrees with a Leonine style decision, they will not hesitate to say.

Capricorn
You find Capricorn a little dull. They are very traditional and conservative, favouring the kinds of muted and subdued colours which are anathema to you. Where you can agree is on the issue of quality, about which you both share a natural appreciation.

Aquarius
Leo and Aquarius are a stressful mixture, tending to work better where members of the opposite sex are concerned. As a Leo, you strive to be different and unusual in your style choices, but here is somebody who does it better than you. Annoyingly, they don't even seem to be trying.

Pisces
Pisceans are dreamy and easy-going, but can feel that life is a little cold if they are left to their own devices. There is nothing they like better than some Leonine warmth to bring them basking to the surface, encouraging the expression of their own creative choices.

Priorities: *cleanliness, order, practicality, service, simplicity, work.*

The typical Virgo

Virgoans are the systems people of the zodiac. They excel behind the scenes and have a talent for organization. Generally modest and retiring, Virgoans strive for perfection – with clarity, efficiency and simplicity placed high on their personal list of priorities. This sign has a particular reputation for cleanliness and for tidiness, although in practice this is often not as extreme as usually depicted. Nevertheless, there certainly will be a preference for order and organization throughout their lives, with an abhorrence of chaos and confusion wherever it occurs.

Virgo's desire for perfection also extends to a general quest for physical and spiritual wellbeing, usually with a special interest in health and dietary matters. Virgoans are hardworking, helpful, dutiful, responsible and focus mainly on the practicalities of life. An excessive desire for perfection is their main failing, since others can easily perceive their largely well-intentioned suggestions as unwarranted criticism. It is as well to remember that Virgoans are actually most severely critical of themselves.

The Virgo home

With Virgo's reputation for order and for hygiene, you can be sure that this home will convey an immediate impression of cleanliness and of tidiness. While in reality the position of other astrological factors does influence such characteristics considerably, most Virgoans do possess a serious loathing for mess and clutter. They will therefore expend great energy in ensuring that everything is organized as efficiently as possible around them. The philosophy of a place for everything is crucial to the average Virgo's peace of mind.

Aside from this, the Virgo home should favour space, light, pale and neutral colours and simple decorative lines. The taste of this sign is simple but not cold. Their excellent eye for detail ensures that even minor features will always receive their full attention. The intelligent use of space would typically be a notable feature, with some novel and ingenious storage ideas. Once an item has served its function, Virgo strives immediately to return it to its customary position.

Characteristics

Favourable

Analytical • modest • helpful • conscientious • meticulous • painstaking • diligent • tidy

Less favourable

Over-analytical • critical • fussy • picky • tense • uneasy • inhibited • wallflower

Sign associations

Symbol The Maiden

Ruling planet Mercury

Day of the week Wednesday

Lucky colours Grey, fawn, mushroom, muted yellows, blues, greens and brown

Lucky number Five

Birthstone Sardonyx

Metal Mercury

Flowers Narcissus, all small brightly coloured flowers, especially in blue or yellow

Trees All nut trees

Regions Brazil, Crete, Greece, Switzerland, Turkey, Uruguay and the West Indies

Cities Athens, Boston, Corinth, Lyons, Paris, Toulouse as well as all spa towns and health resorts

Best partners Capricorn and Taurus

Worst partners Gemini, Pisces and Sagittarius

Ten key factors

crafts
desks
dining rooms
efficiency
embroidery
employment
fitness
gardens
health
light

health

crafts

An earth sign

Since Virgo is an earth sign, there will be a great emphasis on natural fabrics, colours and materials around the home. This applies to walls, floors and furnishings. A clean, spacious and uncluttered feeling is preferred, along with a modern and open-plan approach. This sign particularly suits the Scandinavian style of interior design, where light woods such as beech or birch are used extensively, their paler shades taking precedence over woods with darker tones. Natural light should also feature prominently, with a limited palette of cool and muted colours like white, off-white, grey and even pale blue to continue the natural theme.

ABOVE You favour a straightforward and uncomplicated approach to interior decoration, so your chosen ambience is unfussy and utilitarian. Nonetheless, as an earth sign, your personal comfort is undoubtedly important too.

gardens   embroidery   fitness

Making an entrance

Your home will have a quietly tasteful and understated appearance, since the last thing you like is to draw attention to yourself. Your front door will be either of a plain and light-coloured wood or painted in a muted neutral shade. There will be plenty of windows to admit the maximum amount of light, with those which might compromise privacy either obscured by frosted or intricate stained glass, or covered inside with plain blinds or with a light gauzy material.

The entrance will be extremely clean, with any leaves or litter studiously swept away on a regular basis. There will be a doormat outside, and one inside too, both of which you like visitors to use. A hatstand, umbrella stand and hooks for your coat are the first signs of the organization that lies within.

Living areas

Ideal Virgo living areas are clean, sparingly furnished and should combine modern design trends with a much more traditional perspective. Your ideal flooring would be plain wooden floorboards or a suitable laminate substitute, with decorative rugs here and there to provide greater comfort in specific areas. Alternatively, a natural fibre throughout would also suit you – such as

ABOVE Virgo prefers a low profile, so whilst these stained glass features help to maintain your privacy, they will still appeal to your eye for detail and appreciation of fine craftsmanship.

RIGHT Virgo is probably the most health-conscious sign in the whole zodiac, so a hygienic and orderly kitchen environment in which to prepare your meals is vital.

coir, sisal, hemp or jute – again of prime suitability due to its inherently organic and earthy appearance. Cane, wicker or rattan furniture adds an easy-going and comfortable informality, either left with its natural coloration or painted a matching cool pastel shade. The occasional light-coloured sofa or armchair should then be available for greater relaxation where necessary. Additional furniture of a plain, pale wood should be simple and uncomplicated.

Since Virgo has a particular association with dining areas, a dining table would be a great addition, perhaps next to a bright window overlooking the garden with which you share a particular link. Generally speaking, light levels should be as high as possible, but of a bright and indirect nature rather than glaring and overpowering. Natural light is definitely preferable.

Flooring

Natural flooring is the key. Sanded floorboards in a light-coloured wood and synthetic laminate alternatives are both ideal, with natural fibres such as coir, hemp, jute and sisal as an additional option. Wood also works well in kitchens and bathrooms and can be painted for greater resilience. Otherwise natural resin or rubber flooring provides a good alternative.

Lighting

The Virgo style of decoration most favours natural light, in keeping with the Scandinavian theme, which includes features designed to maximize the reduced levels of light experienced in the winter in that part of the world.

Fabrics and wallpaper

Simple and natural fabrics are the best choices for you. Breezy blues and bright whites help continue the cool and airy theme. Coarser fabrics in natural colours such as hessian, hemp and jute will also find their position within certain specific applications. Voiles and muslin are excellent choices for window coverings, helping to maintain privacy and reduce glare while still letting in the maximum amount of light.

Interior lighting should be bright and not simply restricted to one source. Table lamps, angled lights, stylized standard lamps and recessed ceiling and wall lights will all provide good design opportunities.

Kitchen

Virgo certainly recognizes the importance of a healthy diet. Consequently, the kitchen is likely to be one of the most important areas of your house. However, it is likely to be the scene not of fine wines and the preparation of heavy and extensive banquets but of light and healthy continental-style breakfasts, orange juice, coffee and toast. White would make an ideal predominant colour, with a bright and fresh atmosphere and with lots of useful shelf space on which to display simple ceramic bowls, jugs and other useful yet decorative cooking vessels. Stainless steel suits such an environment too, in terms of appliances and work surfaces as well as the cooking utensils on display.

The floor could be of varnished beech, birch or a synthetic laminate substitute. Otherwise certain rubber or resin options provide a great alternative. These are available in a wide selection of colours that are hardwearing and easy to clean. There should be a simple seating arrangement and, if space permits, a wooden table for all to gather round each morning. Racks for fresh vegetables help round off the picture, with a coffee percolator and fresh herbs grown in ceramic pots up on the window sill.

Art and ornaments

The Virgoan look demands a fairly plain and uncluttered approach. Therefore, you will probably prefer a rather minimalist approach to ornamentation. Tall floor-standing vases containing straight or tortured willow would be ideal, or small bunches of identical flowers used sparingly to stark effect. In addition, since Virgo is associated with crafts, suitable ornaments in other areas of the house would also serve some kind of a practical purpose. Examples here might include china plates, vases and other ceramic accessories.

BELOW The uncluttered and no-nonsense Virgoan bedroom wouldn't suit everyone, but note the use of natural flooring materials adding a further dimension to this uncompromising design scheme.

Bedroom

The ideal Virgo bedroom will probably be rather plain and quite minimalist in its approach, particularly if you are male, since male tastes will often tend towards a greater simplicity than those of their female counterparts. A futon mattress placed on a low frame or directly on the floor is particularly recommended, since such a simple yet contemporary design ideally suits the Virgoan ethos. Natural fibre flooring would again prove an excellent choice and would help to continue the theme from the living areas. If the finish of natural fibre sounds rather harsh, a textured-weave carpet in a plain natural colour would also undoubtedly suit your scheme.

Should your bedroom be in a loft, attic or similar area, it would also prove an ideal candidate for such industrial features as exposed pipes or bare brickwork. The latter option, in particular, helps accentuate the earthy colour scheme and choice of natural materials. Roman blinds or roller-blinds, perhaps in hessian or jute, complement this simple and down-to-earth picture far better than curtains ever could.

ABOVE The stark profile of this washbasin is ideal for your sign. Personal hygiene is important to Virgo, so your bathroom is functional and easy to maintain.

Bathroom

Your bathroom could definitely accommodate some radical design features in order to encourage a truly natural and organic feel. Simplicity should be the order of the day, with white or slightly off-white the predominant colour, and either natural light or ceiling and wall-recessed halogen spotlights providing the necessary illumination.

The modern design of bathroom furniture is often a fundamental and surprising departure from that of the past. Items are pared down to their essence, with shallow dish-like basins on natural-looking shelves and baths owing more to opened cocoons than to previously conventional expectations. Rubber or resin flooring in a natural stone colour ably enhances such an effect, and the addition of a few genuine items from nature, such as bunches of twigs in an interesting vase or piles of large pebbles, can produce an excellent effect. Large wall-mounted mirrors without frames, taps reminiscent of plain waterspouts, and wicker laundry and waste baskets help to finish a look that is remarkably raw yet strangely sophisticated.

Flowers and plants

Architectural plants will prove most complementary to Virgoan styling. Large green foliage plants and striking succulents, are not strictly ruled by Virgo but can all find a place as specimen plants in your design scheme. Cut willow twigs, unusually shaped dried flowers, smaller vases containing many flowers of the same variety and colourful exotic imports like the bird of paradise (Strelitzia) can all be used as prominent features.

Extra room

The perfect extra room for a Virgo would be a conservatory. The combination of informality, an enclosed area surrounded by plants and jutting outwards into your beloved garden, with plenty of glass and a vast amount of natural light, would all serve to help create an area perfect for your relaxation. You love nature, but are not really one of the hardiest, so would definitely enjoy being able to appreciate the natural environment while firmly protected from the worst extremes of the weather. Virgoans are frequently keen gardeners, so a place in which to tend your more delicate specimens, as well as to bring on new seedlings and cuttings, would certainly be greatly valued. The classic Virgoan materials – cane, rattan or wicker furniture, with a natural flooring made of coir, jute, sisal or hemp – would all find excellent application within such an environment. A fan could be installed to keep matters cooler on the hottest days, since you don't really like high temperatures. Translucent and unfussy Roman blinds or roller-blinds would help to bring the temperature down, as well as providing excellent protection from excessive glare throughout the hottest months.

ABOVE You love nature, but you're not so keen on getting dirty, wet and cold. A conservatory is a perfect extra room, so you can admire the outdoors in comfort.

Combining with others

Aries

As a Virgo you prefer a neat and organic design, with an understated and inconspicuous presentation. Aries by contrast is often brash, uses man-made materials and favours an angular approach. There is a need to maintain your own space here, or it is likely that you will soon feel swamped. There are better matches for you.

Taurus

Taurus and Virgo are both earth signs, so you will easily be able to agree on a suitably earthy colour scheme and on a harmonious selection of natural materials. Taurus will prefer more luxury than you, since your own tastes are often rather moderate and spare.

Gemini

You find Gemini infuriating, since they always seem to be dashing around, are forever changing their minds and never seem to settle on one course for very long. You don't understand why they can't just choose a good-looking natural colour scheme and then stick with it.

Cancer

While not totally in tune with one another's objectives, the two of you do understand the other's style quite well. For instance, you may not sympathize entirely with some softer parts of Cancerian design, but you will appreciate its practicality when considering Cancer's lifestyle.

Leo

Leo is too flamboyant and showy for you. Yours is the kind of understated approach which they find very dull. The only way to win Leo over is to convince them of the high fashion connotations involved within a minimalist perspective. They will be expounding it to others soon.

Other Virgo

You would expect two members of the same sign to agree. However, Virgo has a tendency to get caught up with minor details. With two of you together, this tendency is magnified. Unfortunately, this may detract from a harmonious appreciation of the whole.

Libra

Virgo and Libra enjoy a similarly strong approach to the aesthetic components of the modern interior. Perhaps the Virgoan approach is a little more functional and organic, with Libra being slightly more polished and concerned by the finishing touches, but overall the broad similarities are substantial.

Scorpio

Although seemingly not sharing a great deal in terms of their approach towards interior design, there are similarities which these two signs can build upon. These mainly rest upon the significance of detail, a factor of which both signs are particularly fond.

Sagittarius

The Sagittarian home is often quite untidy, a factor which does not augur well so far as Virgo is concerned. Virgo is good with details, Sagittarius with broader concerns. It is not impossible for these two to live well together, if each can concentrate on their own particular strengths.

Capricorn

Capricorn is ambitious and determined, and sets targets years ahead and works towards them. Virgo can certainly appreciate the importance of working for your ideals too. Together you will discuss the layout of your ideal home and will then struggle patiently to implement your plans.

Aquarius

A modest, cautious and conservative Virgo would not seem to have too much in common with wild and wacky Aquarius. However, since simplistic Virgo lines are now contemporary in design terms, there could be rather more to go on than a cursory inspection might suggest.

Pisces

Virgo and Pisces are opposite one another in the zodiac. Although in astrological terms, opposite signs frequently do attract, in this instance it is unlikely to be the case. The Piscean approach to life, living and home decoration is simply too chaotic for poor Virgo to contemplate.

Priorities: *balance, beauty, contrast, harmony, peace, poise.*

The typical Libra

Librans are renowned as the peacemakers of the zodiac. They adore elegance and beauty in their surroundings. They are typically harmonious, easy-going, sociable, diplomatic and are especially concerned with their relationships. Indecision is one of their main failings. Librans function most effectively in close affiliation with others. While this will usually be within a marriage or other similar relationship, close friendships and working relationships can sometimes help fulfil their needs and expectations too.

In practice, the Libran collaborative urge is expressed in two distinct ways. Interpersonal interaction can function either from a co-operative or rather more competitive perspective. Thus certain Librans – at least on initial impressions – are very far from the cordial image traditionally associated with this sign. Combative and confrontational could, in these circumstances, prove to be a much more accurate description. Ultimately, though, the outcome is still the same. Whether through peaceable or more antagonistic dealings with others, the Libran subject is finally able to make up their mind.

The Libra home

Ruled by Venus, Libra is the sign most closely associated with interior design. There is an inherent desire for Librans to surround themselves with beauty, so one might expect the Libran home to represent the pinnacle of excellence in interior decoration. However, in practice Librans enjoy a relaxed, unhurried and quite hedonistic approach to life. They also have a pronounced tendency towards indecision. Together, these characteristics can all too easily cause the home to become a chaotic and ultimately unappealing mixture of many different styles. Arbitrary ornamentation with no strong theme leads all too easily to mess and clutter. Therefore, it is beneficial for the Libran home to be considered from the outset with one clear theme in mind.

Libra has associations with the orient. Bearing this in mind, an appropriate theme might draw heavily on the most notable features of home design in this region. The oriental approach is a strong concept and is spacious, cool and spare. It also carries a marked aesthetic appeal.

Characteristics

Favourable

Diplomatic • sociable • refined • harmonious • charming • cultured • agreeable • easy-going

Less favourable

Indecisive • gullible • frivolous • changeable • weak • two-faced • over compromising • argumentative

Sign associations

Symbol The Scales or Balance

Ruling planet Venus

Day of the week Friday

Lucky colours Pink, most shades of blue and pale and light green

Lucky number Six

Birthstones Jade, sapphire, turquoise, quartz and white marble

Metal Copper

Flowers Hydrangeas, large roses, lilies, violets and all blue flowers

Trees Ash, balm, poplar and grape vines

Regions Argentina, Austria, Burma, Canada, China, Japan, Siberia and Tibet

Cities Antwerp, Copenhagen, Frankfurt, Johannesburg, Lisbon, Nottingham and Vienna

Best partners Aries, Aquarius and Gemini

Worst partners Cancer and Capricorn

Ten key factors

bedrooms
contrast
dressing tables
fashion
flowers
guests
interior decoration
jewellery
upper airy rooms
wardrobes

flowers

contrast

An air sign

Libra as an air sign has a predominantly intellectual approach to life. In common with the other air signs, Librans place great value on human relationships. There is nothing that a Libran likes better than a small informal dinner party with a few close friends. Although natural designers with excellent taste and an innate sense of colour and form, they will always be dissatisfied with their own work if they are unable to share it with others. This could mean discussing their initial ideas with a partner or colleague, or might extend to asking a few friends around to help with their implementation. Planning and executing matters purely for themselves would seem a very hollow and lonely undertaking indeed.

ABOVE Libra is linked with the orient and those born under this sign value an aesthetic approach. Being rather indecisive, you'll appreciate the strict guidelines that an oriental scheme entails.

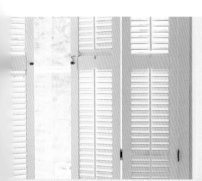

upper airy rooms

interior decoration

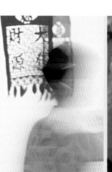

fashion

Making an entrance

Decorated in a combination of various oriental styles, the first impression on entering your ideal home is one of calmness, clarity and serenity. Regardless of the home's exterior, on entry a visitor will be transported into another world. The oriental theme works well in almost any type of modern home, but may require something of a rethink with older or more country-style properties.

In order to begin the transition from outside to inside, a few ornamental touches around your front door would assist this process. Oriental motifs and windchimes, interesting statues and the intelligent use of gravel, stone or water would all prove useful. Plants such as dwarf conifers, potted bonsai or a Japanese maple (acer) would also prepare visitors for the prominent themes to come.

Once inside, the overall impression is minimalist and low, with the furniture levels kept close to the floor. Accessories are also few in number. For areas where clutter is likely to abound, a simple arrangement of screening helps prevent this spare initial impression being spoiled.

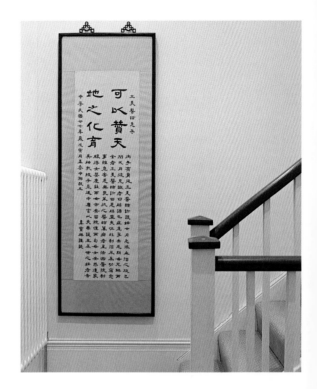

ABOVE The imaginative use of oriental symbolism helps to prepare the visitor for their journey into a new world of design and form. Windchimes and exterior planting have a similar impact.

Living areas

The essence of the oriental look involves combining very pale walls with very dark furniture to form a striking contrast. Thus in your ideal home the walls will be simply lined and then painted either white or off-white. They will largely be plain, perhaps with only the occasional picture or wall-hanging to continue and to enhance the eastern theme. Mirrors hung in dark corners help to echo Feng Shui principles. Libran colours, such as pale pink, green or blue, can be used for variety if the overall impression appears too stark.

The flooring in such an area should certainly be natural. Varnished wooden floorboards or natural fibres such as coir, hemp, jute and sisal are all perfect choices for you. Those who cannot live without carpeting should select one in a natural colour and with a woven or ribbed texture, since this conveys a natural appearance without any of the possible drawbacks that are linked to alternative products.

Dark wood furniture completes the picture, with low-level tables in wenge or black ash. Chairs should also be dark, maybe in steel and black plastic or in black leather. A square and plainly upholstered white sofa, with a couple of contrasting scatter cushions only, is then suited to greater relaxation.

Flooring

Natural flooring is usually your preference. Wood is probably the easiest option, ranging from sanded and varnished floorboards, through painted floorboards, to the genuinely authentic bamboo laminate. Other goodchoices are natural fibres such as coir, hemp, jute, seagrass and sisal. Alternatively, you could use a textured or woven carpet to mimic a natural appearance. Natural slate, or a modern synthetic imitation, would certainly prove eminently suitable in bathroom and kitchen areas.

Fabrics and wallpaper

Wallpaper is generally not for you. Walls should simply be lined and painted with a plain white or off-white emulsion. You can then use wall-hangings reminiscent of the Far East to add emphasis, with silk being particularly linked both to Libra and to this style of decoration. Otherwise, natural fibres such as cotton and linen are excellent, combined with scattered patterns using natural motifs.

Lighting

Libra loves soft romantic lighting, so there is great scope within the oriental theme for using paper lanterns indoors and paper screens at windows, in order to diffuse some of the harsher elements of both natural and artificial light. Woven blinds, white or wooden Venetian blinds, straight hung sheer fabric panels and floating muslin at windows could all have a similar effect. Low-level lighting placed on the floor will contribute greatly to the overall ambience, without ever threatening to outshine or to dominate the otherwise simple décor.

Kitchen

Libra's symbol is the Scales or the Balance. Symbolically, your quest is to find a compromise between two opposing extremes. Therefore, the two-tone theme that begins in your living areas, where the contrast between light and dark is used creatively and to dramatic effect, finds further application in your kitchen. Here the flooring can also be wooden, provided it is sealed adequately beforehand to make it truly water-resistant. For those wishing authentically to continue the oriental theme, bamboo laminate really has to be the ultimate

ABOVE Librans are always attempting to balance opposing viewpoints. From a design perspective this yields some interesting results, when contrast is deliberately emphasized in the Libran kitchen for example.

choice. This has the added advantage of coping better with kitchen conditions than most similar wooden floors. Black slate would also be an excellent option for providing contrast with white walls. Various man-made flooring materials can produce a similar effect.

Slate or granite and synthetic equivalents are subsequently ideal for your kitchen work surfaces. Natural dark wood, bamboo or white laminate units add to this picture, depending on your other design choices made so far. Contrasting plain black and white china, wall tiles and accessories serve to round matters off in a similar vein.

Bedroom

Simplicity is the key for your bedroom. A futon bed or more conventional mattress, placed close to the floor and with no headboard, would ideally continue the oriental theme. A natural wood or bamboo laminate floor provides continuity with the existing Libran living areas. Natural-fibre flooring could also be employed, though, if you are seeking greater variety in your design choices. Otherwise, plain rugs with striking motifs and ribbed carpet provide more comfort where necessary. Wooden floorboards painted white are always a bold statement within such a context.

Additional bedroom furniture should be kept to a minimum. Basic wicker chairs are much better in this context, where upholstered items would look out of place. Rattan tables and other furnishings, with wooden or cane blinds for the windows, are far more suitable than fussier seating and storage alternatives. A selection of sisal baskets provide further options for storage and for ensuring that the room stays clutter-free, although undoubtedly a good selection of cupboards and wardrobes will prove essential if you are to maintain such an ideal.

Bathroom

Continuing the oriental theme most effectively, the perfect central feature for your bathroom is a large sunken bath, where you can lie back and luxuriate at floor level. Although such radical design features are not possible in every home, it may still be feasible to compromise with a simple low bath accessed by means of a series of purposely accentuated steps.

ABOVE The extensive use of plain black and white serves constantly to highlight contrasting extremes. A futon bed and natural fibre flooring continue the oriental theme into the Libran bedroom.

Art and ornaments

Less is definitely more where art and ornaments are concerned. Examples of Chinese calligraphy can make excellent framed pictures or striking wall-hangings, as can floral themes involving orchids, lotus flowers or bamboo. Otherwise the occasional and appropriately styled ceramic in black, white or a contrasting colour can be used to great effect, although it is always important to keep things sparse for maximum impact.

Suitable flooring would be wooden, bamboo laminate, slate or their equivalent synthetic alternatives – depending on the flooring methods used elsewhere. All these materials contrast well with those familiar white walls. For those seeking greater variety, smooth limestone or ceramic floor tiles also work well for you. The bathroom furniture would comprise units in dark wood, or bamboo, plain white ceramic or man-made granite equivalents. Paper screens, bamboo or seagrass room dividers can be usefully employed to keep any obvious bathroom clutter safely out of view.

ABOVE The floor-to-ceiling use of light wood or bamboo laminate tiling provides a striking alternative to plainer wall treatments. A few strategic accessories add an unmistakably oriental feel.

Flowers and plants

Lilies and African violets are both ruled by Libra and would make excellent selections when placed in a few choice locations. Otherwise flowering orchids of the phalaenopsis group, the bare red stems of the dogwood *Salix alba*, some bamboo or bamboo stems and a couple of bonsai specimens would all prove in keeping with the themes of your home. A Japanese maple (acer) or evergreen conifer might prove particularly effective as the bonsai.

LEFT The strict guidelines of a Libran theme mean plenty of cupboard space to keep things clear. Most Librans love fashion so ample wardrobes are a must.

Extra room

In many ways, the minimalist oriental approach is ideal for Libra. It provides a strong and clearly defined theme for a person who loves beautiful things but has terrible trouble making decisions. Choices are fewer with such a strict scheme, and are helpfully limited in their scope, while in the mean time no compromises will ever need to be made from an aesthetic perspective.

The only trouble is that you love clothes. Libra is the sign most closely associated with fashion and jewellery. It rules dressing tables, cosmetics and wardrobes. So where will these Libran accoutrements find a place within such an organized domestic environment? The answer lies inside the classic Libran extra room – the walk-in wardrobe.

Literally a wardrobe that is almost big enough to be a room, the Libran walk-in wardrobe has rails and hooks for larger clothes, drawers for smaller items and plentiful shelf space for all those items in between. Carefully hidden behind a plain white or slatted black contrasting door, here you will be free to pick and choose, and to leave items in as much of a state of disarray as the mood takes you. At the same time, you are able to maintain a beautiful home too.

Combining with others

Aries

An excellent match. Aries is encouraged to take life easier from time to time and not to try doing everything at once. The Libran is inspired by Aries certainty and by their proactive attitude and approach. Librans also help to round the edges on a rather more brutal design scheme.

Taurus

Although both ruled by Venus and thus usually blessed with excellent taste, Taurus is primarily concerned with personal comfort while Libra is mainly linked with beauty and with social interaction. Thus there are still some important differences between these two in terms of decoration and design choices.

Gemini

Libra and Gemini should agree on many design principles, although from time to time you may find Gemini's energy to be a little scattered. They in turn could find you a little set in your ways, so there is probably quite a lot which you can learn from each other.

Cancer

Although you admire Cancer's reverence for the family and their dedication to the home, their rather fussy and traditional approach really isn't your thing at all. Still, you can definitely appreciate the importance of other people in creating a happy domestic situation. On this basis, you can move forward together.

Leo

Libra and Leo are a happy mix, with Libra looking adoringly at Leo's decorative decisions and with Leo basking in the attention which they are sure they so obviously deserve. If Leo could encourage Libra to develop their own decorative talents, then this would be the best situation of all.

Virgo

There are many similarities between the two of you, since you are both drawn easily to a stylish and a minimal approach. However, Virgo is possibly a little earthy for your liking and they may feel that your tastes are somewhat flowery. Nevertheless, there is still a lot of common ground.

Other Libra

An excellent combination for aesthetic appreciation, but not the best for decision-making. Should we have carpet or natural flooring? Maybe the latter, but should we opt for coir, hemp, jute, sisal or seagrass? Then, of course, sanded floorboards are lovely too...and aren't ceramic tiles great?

Scorpio

Libra and Scorpio don't have a great deal in common. Librans need to keep their design schemes simple in order to avoid cluttering up their life. Scorpio is the opposite and likes lots of intrigue, epitomized by busy décor and by loads of secret nooks and crannies. Separate rooms, perhaps?

Sagittarius

Libra and Sagittarius get along well, although Sagittarius might be a little too messy for Libra's refined sensibilities. Sagittarius is an uncomplicated soul and will think that you are great regardless, although it has to be said that scrupulous cleaning has never been their strongest point.

Capricorn

You are willing to try different ideas from other parts of the world and to appreciate how other cultures can improve upon a traditional perspective. Capricorns are usually far too dour and stern for you, in terms both of their personal expression and of their conservative approach to interior design.

Aquarius

As an air sign you are well aware that unusual and sometimes revolutionary ideas are the driving force behind the latest developments in fashion, design and construction materials. Aquarius is always coming up with new ideas and is always ready to try new things. A good match.

Pisces

Both Libra and Pisces appreciate beauty, although your own aesthetic sensibilities will tend to follow more clear-cut and practical lines. You can certainly appreciate how stunning all that wonderfully floating gauze and muslin looks, but to live with it from day to day could seem more trouble than it is worth.

Priorities: *privacy, intensity, secrecy, passion, regeneration.*

The typical Scorpio

Scorpios are deep and strong, intuitive and powerful, intense and very private people. They have excellent powers of observation and possess an astute understanding of human nature. They make the best of friends and the worst of enemies. A Scorpio will unswervingly support a colleague through times of trouble, but once crossed will feel obliged to wreak a fearsome revenge. Otherwise they are passionate in everything they do. They feel that every activity worth undertaking is worth commanding their full attention.

Scorpios enjoy a reputation for being sexually active and are extremely jealous and possessive. However, they are just as likely to refrain from sexual activity completely, purposely avoiding such encounters because of the strong and complex feelings they are certain will be raised. By turns, Scorpio can be as hot as fire and as cold as ice. While imbued with the same sensitive emotional nature common to all the water signs, they will differ in favouring attack as the most effective means of defence.

The Scorpio home

Scorpio is a sign which is particularly associated with mystery, intrigue and secrecy and this is often reflected in their choice of furnishings. Scorpios always value their privacy, so if you are invited into a Scorpio home you should consider yourself to be very honoured indeed. This is not a sign which suits a minimalist approach to home decoration. Walking into a room and cataloguing every item with one brief yet penetrating stare does not represent much of a challenge to the Scorpion's investigative spirit.

Scorpios like a lot of interest, such as plenty of handcrafted items with appealing facets and textures and many different smaller areas within one room or home. This variety and sense of intrigue serves to attract and then to maintain their interest and attention. Light and shadow can be used creatively in furthering such an impression. Scorpio is linked to darkness and to the night, so that even in the daytime we should expect reduced light levels in many areas of the house. Shadowy corners encourage stronger souls to investigate further.

Characteristics

Favourable

Deep • intense • resolute • powerful • loyal • discerning • intuitive • subtle

Less favourable

Jealous • vindictive • vengeful • secretive • suspicious • pitiless • twisted • malicious

Sign associations

Symbol The Scorpion

Ruling planet Pluto

Day of the week Tuesday

Lucky colours Deep red, maroon and brown

Lucky number Nine

Birthstones Opal, ruby and bloodstone

Metals Iron and steel

Flowers Heather, dark red flowers, especially geraniums and rhododendrons

Trees Blackthorn, bushy and thorn-bearing trees in general

Regions Bavaria, Korea, Morocco, Norway, Queensland, Syria and the Transvaal

Cities Baltimore, Cincinnati, Liverpool, Newcastle, New Orleans and Washington DC

Best partners Cancer, Taurus and Pisces

Worst partners Gemini, Leo and Aquarius

Ten key factors

aroma
bathrooms
darkness
lavatories
ponds
purification
puzzles
recycling
renovation
synthetic materials

aroma

darkness

A water sign

Scorpio shares the emotional attributes common to the water signs. You are subjective in your outlook, predominantly emotional in your response to life, possess good intuition and could never be described as shallow. However, before the discovery of Pluto in 1930, this sign was considered to be jointly ruled by Mars, a clear indication of the much more fiery and proactive approach to life that helps to differentiate Scorpio from the other water signs.

When it comes to colour, Scorpio is closely linked with fiery colours such as dark reds and maroon, in preference to the blues and greens. A strong design theme will also definitely be preferred.

ABOVE A sumptuous North African or Middle Eastern theme is perfect for the Scorpio home, with purposely reduced levels of light creating areas of shadow and intrigue.

synthetic materials

bathrooms

purification

Making an entrance

Visitors may have trouble finding the Scorpio residence and, when they do, there will be little about it to distinguish it from its surroundings. Privacy is an obsession for you, so your home could be hidden from sight behind a high wall, fence or hedge, situated at the end of a cul-de-sac or a long drive surrounded by trees. Basement living is also ideal. Even in the daytime, the curtains may well be drawn.

The exterior of the house will have been designed to blend in, with a formidable alarm system, gate and other features warning of dire consequences for those who enter uninvited. A rather less recommended approach would be to leave the front of the house uncared for, with the brambles growing thickly and with the windows dirty, in order to give the impression that nobody is at home.

Living areas

Once inside, it is a very different environment, a timeless haven of mystery and intrigue, an evocatively scented and shadowy world strongly influenced by the souks and kasbahs of the Arabian nights. Behind the heavily textured and hand-embroidered curtains, a mainly North African and Middle Eastern theme predominates, with influences reminiscent of Morocco, Tunisia, Egypt, Turkey and the Levant.

The floor will be covered in richly decorated rugs perhaps of Berber and Bedouin provenance, with Turkish kilims and similar thick and exotic tapestries hanging from the walls. A low coffee table, ornate daybed and matching cabinet or sideboard are all intricately carved from aged dark brown

Fabrics and wallpaper

Scorpio fabrics are heavy and textured, and walls are best painted or covered with tapestries and ethnic wall-hangings. Your uncompromising approach also makes you a prime candidate for a rough and textured plaster finish, which, bearing in mind your desire to cut through to the heart of things, could even in certain situations be left totally unpainted. Fabrics should aim for a rich but subdued look. Bold, geometric and even bejewelled patterns are particularly in keeping with the ethnic North African theme.

hardwoods such as teak, mahogany and iroko. Several of these items appear to be antique and are doubtless extremely rare. They probably feature prominent and complex fretwork in their design. To encourage complete relaxation, the daybed will be covered with large and luxurious cushions in a selection of lavish but restrained colours.

For additional seating, you might have ornate leather pouffes on the floor, intricately stitched and decorated by hand. Additional ornamentation will be extensive throughout, maybe with a large ornamental waterpipe taking pride of place in one corner.

Flooring

Flooring can follow a couple of main themes throughout your home. Firstly, there are tiles for potentially wet areas such as kitchens and bathrooms; these could be terracotta, handmade clay pammets from the Mediterranean, or hand-painted with bold geometric images for a really powerful impact. Thick ethnic rugs or kilims are definitely the preferred option for the remaining areas, once more in the richer and deeper shades of red, maroon and brown.

ABOVE The Scorpio kitchen contains plenty of intriguing ethnic artefacts, sourced from obscure and inaccessible locations all over the world. Your eye is inevitably drawn to investigate further.

Lighting

Lighting in the Scorpio home is likely to be subdued. Thick textured curtains and improvised drapes, wooden shutters and ethnic-style blinds help keep natural daylight muted and low. Wherever possible, you usually prefer candlelight. Ornate glass, wrought-iron, brass and silver lanterns from around the world are used to enhance its entrancing effects, casting fascinating shadows around the room and attracting attention to even the most mundane of areas.

Kitchen

Scorpio is not a sign for whom food assumes great importance. The Scorpion can go for long periods without any food at all. You often like to eat in seclusion and to keep your dietary habits to yourself. Thus the kitchen is unlikely to form any kind of major focal point in your home, but rather should

be decorated in a complementary style to ensure continuity. This might also perhaps engender rather greater use than otherwise would be the case.

A fairly straightforward wooden kitchen in a medium tone is likely to form the best compromise between establishing a friendly ambience and creating unwelcome maintenance. Minimalism is not recommended, so the atmosphere should be cosy, giving the impression of textural and tonal diversity and of lots of different areas to explore.

If the kitchen is large enough, a medium- to dark-toned wooden table and chairs would aid greater social interaction and a more prolonged use of the kitchen area. A few ethnic artefacts such as gourds, baskets or carved wooden utensils could be hung up to provide a link with the living areas. Splashbacks in hand-painted tiles and with abstract Islamic designs would serve to enhance the ethnic theme.

Bedroom

Opulence and luxury can really go to town in your bedroom. Because of this sign's association with both passion and seclusion, the bedroom is a

Art and ornaments

Ethnic artefacts are particularly suited to the Scorpio look. Try to cover the room with items either hanging or perched on every available space, aiming for an impression of a veritable Aladdin's cave. For example, think about what can be done with ornate bangles and bracelets, strings of miniature silver bells and small, exotic looking statuettes. Stone or ceramic incense burners and mirrors with brass, hole-punched or embossed-tin surrounds, make perfect accessories. A couple of large ornamental urns would complete the picture.

A fire sign

In common with other members of this element, Sagittarius is characterized by action, initiative and energy. Progressing through the zodiac there is a gradual evolution in the depth and complexity with which each sign is associated. When considering Sagittarius, it is therefore apparent that intellectual stimulation and development are far more prominent expectations.

Sagittarius is associated with dark blue, violet and purple. This demonstrates how blue now assumes a greater impact on the fiery colour palette. Blue also corresponds with the element of air and confers logic, intellect and a cerebral approach.

ABOVE The ideal Sagittarian home has a comfortable and a lived-in feel, with plentiful reading matter to keep you stimulated intellectually and with a large open fire as the central focus.

religion

durability

personal space

Making an entrance

Somehow it seems that your residence has grown and evolved in a rather organic manner. No particular style has been followed slavishly. The impression is homely and relaxed and is reminiscent of a countryside lifestyle. Clearly, certain themes were once observed in decoration, but these have now been augmented and modified by an eclectic mixture of personal preferences along the way. There is a slightly worn and lived-in appearance, which instantly places the visitor at ease.

Otherwise, this part of your house is probably none too tidy. Your outdoor lifestyle means that the entrance hall functions as something of a buffer zone, withstanding the worst of the elements that you and your animals bring in. There is wooden panelling to dado level, a sturdy mat, coathooks, and somewhere for your boots.

Living areas

The centre point of your main room is a large open fire, where a cheerful blaze burns merrily during the colder parts of the year. There is a large hearth, with fire-irons, a well-used coal scuttle and a stack of ash logs. More logs are stored in some rustic-looking baskets to one side.

A similar effect can be achieved in more modern residences by using imitation 'real' fires run on gas or electricity. A mantelpiece above the fire has an unusual and eclectic mixture of ethnic wooden carvings, with pewter statuettes of various deities from exotic religions around the world. The dust lies a little noticeably on these, as does various other debris on the wooden floor, although not sufficient to prove unhygienic. Nobody seems worried about its presence, in any case.

Your seating comprises a large settee and a couple of armchairs in a circular arrangement. These are of good quality and are still extremely comfortable, but now are covered by throws in order to disguise a little wear. Somehow the visitor feels an overwhelming impulse to kick off their shoes and talk a while. There is no television, but a large and well-stocked bookcase shows that reading is an important activity during your quieter moments.

Flooring

Easy maintenance, resilience and a natural feel are again key factors when it comes to your choice of flooring. Sanded and varnished floorboards with ethnic and oriental rugs make a great choice for living areas; otherwise use natural alternatives such as coir and seagrass. Ceramic or terracotta tiles are ideal for areas such as kitchens and bathrooms, and there are natural stone options like slate, sandstone or quarry tiles for a really 'outdoor' experience.

Lighting

Natural daylight should be maximized wherever possible. Window treatments should be uncomplicated with simple curtains, wooden blinds or slatted wooden shutters providing you with the necessary privacy where needed.

ABOVE You pass into the friendly environs of the Sagittarian home through a kind of buffer zone that prevents the worst elements of an outdoor lifestyle from entering unbidden.

Fabrics and wallpaper

The Sagittarian home can easily stand a wide variety of fabrics, textures and wall coverings. Mixing and matching is probably the key, giving the impression of a setting that has grown over time rather than being too rigorously planned. Fabrics will generally need to be quite hardwearing, so it would be better to choose resilient cottons and linens rather than anything daintier.

Interior lighting is likely to be fairly traditional in approach. Standard lamps and table lamps that feature fabric shades drawn from the Sagittarian style options will prove more in keeping than slicker modern alternatives.

ABOVE The Sagittarian kitchen contains an eclectic arrangement of furniture, from many different sources over the years. The impression is warm and welcoming, immediately putting you at your ease.

Kitchen

Food is not an obsession for Sagittarians, but you do enjoy the good things in life. This includes rich food, fine wines and good living. You often have lots of friends, so enjoy eating and drinking together as a means of spreading good will. While by no means the centre of your existence, the kitchen is likely to prove an important room in your home.

Ideally, the Sagittarian kitchen should follow the same friendly, spacious, yet moderately cluttered approach that characterizes the remainder of your home. Completely disregarding the environment in which the kitchen is actually located, a modern yet rural theme will best suit your rangy and outdoor character. Older pine units and medium-toned oak should be favoured for kitchen furniture. Terracotta, slate or quarry tiles help to promote a natural impression for the floor.

Where space permits, a large dining table and chairs would serve to encourage conversation. A pine or oak dresser in a simple style displays a mixed selection of china in harmonizing shades. Pots and pans are hung around, with kitchen appliances maintaining a fairly retro feel. Stainless steel would look rather incongruous in such a situation – copper, brass and enamel are far more in keeping with the Sagittarian style.

Bedroom

Your bedroom is not only a place to sleep, it is a space in which to luxuriate, to spend long winter evenings drinking fine red wine and watching classic movies on TV. It is the setting for lengthy weekend mornings with buttered toast and the Sunday papers. By using rich autumnal colours for the walls and curtains, you can promote a more restful atmosphere, while the natural and outdoor symbolism is maintained.

Textured seagrass or ribbed coir flooring sets the tone. This is accompanied by an aged pine, oak or wrought-iron bedstead. Chequered woollen blankets are thrown over the bed. Free-standing storage in a medium-toned or painted wood is much more in keeping with such a setting than alternative fitted options. Furniture can be drawn from a variety of

ABOVE The Sagittarian interest in the higher mind finds expression in this unusual metal sculpture. The zebra throw is a reminder of faraway places.

Art and ornaments

Remembering the Sagittarian association with philosophy and religion, it would not be entirely unexpected for the art and ornamentation in your home to carry sacred and religious overtones. Exact symbolism might range from reproductions of early Christian icons and Buddhist statuettes through to ornate castings of ancient Egyptian and Hindu deities. This sign is particularly associated with pewter.

sources and would probably best be purchased second-hand, its slightly worn appearance fitting well with the relaxed and easy atmosphere. A solid chest of drawers and large wooden wardrobe, together with a conventional dressing table, linen chest and perhaps wicker storage baskets, then complement the picture as space permits.

Bathroom

Your bathroom is both warm and comfortable. It could not really be described as tidy, and gives something of the impression of a work in progress. It is light and airy with a couple of hardy plants placed in suitable locations. It also smells great with plenty of bath salts, bubble bath and aromatherapy bath oils on display.

The bath itself, sink and toilet are in plain white. They all have brass fittings and there is a distressed wooden toilet seat. A large old-fashioned sink and dramatic free-standing roll-top bath would be ideal if circumstances allow. There is a bathroom cabinet in aged pine or a similar medium-coloured wood. There are matching shelves on which bath paraphernalia is stored openly for easy access.

The bathroom walls are of a rough plaster painted in a light pastel shade. This again reflects the colours of nature, but now in a fresher, more spring-like and energizing way. The floor is covered in plain and slightly off-white ceramic tiles, to continue the softer and more natural tones. For extra comfort, there are fabric bathmats placed around the toilet, sink and bath.

Flowers and plants

Ideal plants for your home will also need to be quite resilient since, while they are undoubtedly fond of their houseplants, the average Sagittarian is not always there to ensure that their needs are met regularly in terms of light, heat and water. Cut flowers and striking dried flowers are therefore effective alternatives to live specimens, although carnations and pinks are both particularly associated with this sign and can sometimes be raised indoors.

LEFT The Sagittarian bathroom gives the impression of a work in progress. The plainly painted or bare plaster walls are the perfect complement to distressed woodwork and attractively aged bathroom furniture.

Extra room

Sagittarians are always interested in new ideas and in unusual schools of thought. You have a great tolerance for others' views and are endlessly fascinated by comparative religion and philosophy. Although you won't necessarily agree with another's perspective, you will wish to learn about their concepts and ideas. You will defend the right of the individual to hold their own beliefs and to disseminate their views to others.

For many hundreds of years, great thinkers have expounded their ideas in book form. Since Sagittarius also rules publishing, all Sagittarians possess considerable reverence for the printed word and for books in particular. The ideal extra room in the Sagittarian household is thus the library.

Ideally, this room would be lined from floor to ceiling with oak shelves. These groan under the weight of hundreds of books, ranging in age and size from battered leather-bound first editions, through antique pamphlets and hardbacks, to an extensive selection of the latest paperback novels and reference works. A couple of ancient leather armchairs and a reading table provide the ideal situation for the peaceful perusal of the library's contents. The floor may be carpeted or made of natural stone, but in either case is decorated with a selection of exotic oriental rugs.

ABOVE Electronic media and the internet may be gaining ground, but for you there's no substitute for a good hefty tome. The printed word will never die while Sagittarians are around.

Combining with others

Aries
You certainly appreciate one another's views when it comes to interior decoration. After all, life's too short to worry about trivialities and you won't be afraid to discuss important things. As fire signs, your outlook is really quite similar, with Sagittarius offering an extra dimension to the brasher Aries approach.

Taurus
Taurus loves comfort and luxurious surroundings, Sagittarius would rather be travelling or walking the dogs. However, both signs have the potential for self-indulgence in a big way. Although not an ideal mix, should fate fling these two together this is at least one area on which they can both agree.

Gemini
This combination occurs regularly and is often very happy too. A mature Sagittarian grounds the mutable Gemini by providing a consistent design scheme and a stable home life. Gemini can easily be distracted and might otherwise have found this rather more difficult to maintain.

Cancer
Not a classic combination, but one which occurs too frequently to be pure coincidence. Sagittarius is often out and Cancer is fondest of staying at home. Thus the decorative scheme will be largely Cancerian, with Sagittarian items dotted here and there which they have thoughtfully brought home from their travels.

Leo
A pure fire sign combination, this one is classically considered to be a good match. Leo thrives on appreciation and has to be the biggest and the best. Sagittarius loves things which are big and grand too, so will indulgently encourage and applaud the Leo's enthusiastic creations.

Virgo
Although you share a similar interest in natural materials, it is probable that Sagittarius finds the Virgoan design scheme to be rather dull. Ideally, you would like to use a lot more colour and to juxtapose some interesting artefacts from around the world.

Libra
This could be a good mix, since Libra appreciates firm views on many subjects, not simply interior decoration and design. Although they will usually go along with whatever you suggest, they might prove rather clingy. They certainly won't appreciate it when you go off travelling on your own.

Scorpio
Although not a classic mixture, the two of you can share a joint fascination with ethnic art and decoration. However, Scorpio is very careful with possessions and you are much more carefree, clumsy and rumbustious. It won't take many mishaps for some harsh words to be exchanged. You'll soon forget, but they won't.

Other Sagittarius
Two Sagittarians together will certainly have a very good time. However, all the partying could make it hard to further any decorative options at all. Actually, in reality this could also be your strength. Why not ask a bunch of friends around to join you in a decorating party?

Capricorn
These two must have something to teach each other, because it is a combination you will sometimes find. On a good day Capricorn is a stabilizing influence, but on a bad day they seem restrictive, depressing and deadly dull. Usually it is the latter scenario that predominates, so this isn't really a recommended mix..

Aquarius
The two of you have a lot in common. Aquarius is definitely intrigued by your countryside lifestyle, especially when it includes the addition of more esoteric decorative factors and an alternative, slightly ethnic approach. Aquarius favours new technology more than you do, but mainly you should get on very well.

Pisces
You don't have much in common with Pisces. You are sure that those gauzy window dressings and translucent fabrics are lovely, but in reality you couldn't be bothered. You muse about the impact of your wellingtons, wet dogs and half a kilo of mud. Not for you really, is it?

Priorities: *permanence, reliability, solidity, structure, tradition.*

The typical Capricorn

Capricorns are serious, responsible, prudent, reliable, cautious, conservative, reserved and down to earth. They are generally ambitious, determined and hardworking, often with a major focus on achievement and career. Capricorns typically experience much hardship in early life, but flower with maturity and often rise to positions of prominence and respect. They are hard on themselves and always feel the need to be busy and productive. They can thus find it rather difficult to relax.

Capricorn makes an excellent provider from a material perspective and tends to place practicalities above purely emotional concerns. This can be great in terms of coping with life's inevitable ups and downs, but generally proves rather detrimental to a closer emotional rapport. Nevertheless, these saturnine characters are actually very sensitive and really want others to think the best of them. Pessimism and depression are constant companions, yet in spite of their overly serious outlook a biting dry sense of humour and exceptional intuition are frequently to be noted.

The Capricorn home

It is not a good idea to call unexpectedly at the Capricorn home. Its occupants will be busy – because they work from home, because they have a pressing deadline and have brought work home, or because they are involved with what they consider to be the many responsibilities of running their lives. They will be concentrating on the tasks in hand and won't be happy to be interrupted.

It isn't that they aren't pleased to see you, just that there is so much else they need to do. They will be brusque rather than impolite or rude, but it will be clear that you are intruding. Essentially it would be better to arrange a date some way in advance, or you could wait until you are invited, although you must be prepared to be patient. Then your hosts will have had the opportunity to prepare themselves and to ready their home for visitors. It may not appear much different to you, but it will look very different to them. They will have been to so much trouble that you will be very welcome indeed.

Characteristics

Favourable

Ambitious • assiduous • conservative • sensible • constant • self-disciplined • responsible • realistic

Less favourable

Pessimistic • calculating • mean • miserable • inhibited • rigid • strict • stern

Sign associations

Symbol The Sea Goat

Ruling planet Saturn

Day of the week Saturday

Lucky colours Dark brown, dark green, grey and black

Lucky number Eight

Birthstones Dark sapphires, black pearl, onyx and jet

Metal Lead

Flowers Amaranthus, black poppies, heartsease, hemlock, ivy, nightshade and pansy

Trees Aspen, elm, pine, quince, yew and willow

Regions Afghanistan, Albania, Bosnia, Bulgaria, India, Lithuania, Mexico and the UK

Cities Brandenberg, Brussels, Delhi, Ghent, Mexico City, Oxford and Port Said

Best partners Taurus, Virgo and often Aries

Worst partners Libra

Ten key factors

bricks
coal
gates
granite
leather and all animal hides
limestone
pottery
sculpture
stone
wood

wood

leather

An earth sign

Capricorn favours practical values, principles and materials that are timeless, and is traditional and conservative in taste and outlook. Capricorn is a staunch supporter of hard work and most appreciates those things that have been a struggle to achieve. A palette of browns, blacks and dark greens is ideal.

Stone is a favoured material, since although difficult to work, it yields the most enduring results. Capricorn also has a strong sense of structure and form, so is actually linked with all structural materials. Exposed brickwork or beams could thus be particularly appropriate in the Capricorn home, with the latter also often indicative of the age and durability which this sign so reveres.

ABOVE Your sign rules tradition and the orthodox. You favour a conservative approach to interior decoration, so to replace carpet with white painted floorboards is a radical new departure.

sculpture   bricks   stone

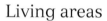

the capricorn home – room by room

Making an entrance

Capricorns are fond of tradition and favour tried and tested decorative formulae. You choose hardwearing materials and a limited palette of plain colours, with simple black and white proving very popular. Therefore as a visitor enters the Capricorn home they are struck by the atmosphere of quality, but also by an impression which pays considerable homage to values past.

Underfoot, your hallway is ideally tiled in a chequered diamond pattern with small matt ceramic tiles in black and white, relaying an impression of a bygone age and of craftsmanship skills that are harder to come by nowadays. There is a bulky traditional-style radiator, painted black. A stained-glass window is above the front door, with dark wooden panelling inside to the height of the dado rail. A gilded mirror on the wall enables you to check your appearance before visitors arrive. The hallway is rather cold, since you are perennially on an economy drive.

Living areas

In climates and seasons which permit, the focal point of your living area will be the traditional open fire. The fire assumes greater presence when surrounded by an ornate mantelpiece in stone, wood or even painted concrete. Both coal and wood are ruled by Capricorn and help to build a wonderful blaze. Flame-effect gas or electric fires are a good alternative in more modern homes. Carved corbels, a cast-iron grate, brass accessories and tiled surrounds all add to this picture of quality.

In terms of seating, your ideal sofa would be a large button-back Chesterfield. This could be in black or brown leather, or in a wonderfully aged red. Accompanied by winged high-back armchairs upholstered in a different colour, this seating arrangement is linked together by ensuring that the legs of each item are finished in a similar style.

A plain carpet would best suit the Capricorn living area, in a light colour such as cream, and overlaid in prime locations with high-quality Persian rugs. Look for top-of-the-range carpets, since their quality will fit in perfectly with Capricorn's style.

Flooring

Most varieties of flooring will find their place somewhere in your home. Luxurious carpets will suit the bedroom and the living areas, with Persian rugs an important addition for the former. Ceramic tiles are ideal for the hall and the bathroom and a dark natural stone should be used for the kitchen. In addition, for larger reception rooms, parquet flooring is a great wooden alternative, with its exclusive nature and the difficulties involved in its installation both an added attraction for you.

Lighting

Window treatments are generally luxurious. Think curtain valances, swags, tails and tiebacks in intricate patterns or luxurious heavy materials such as velvet

ABOVE The black and white tiling featured in this Capricorn hallway suits entirely from the perspective of its traditional conservatism, its hard-wearing nature and its uncompromising geometric pattern.

Fabrics and wallpaper

Hessian is linked with Capricorn, an association ascribed as a consequence of this fabric's rough and meagre nature. However, there is little scope for hessian within your home, where the emphasis rests rather more on a time-honoured sense of quality and style. Fortunately, leather is also linked with your sign, and its exclusive nature is likely to prove far more in keeping.

ABOVE A traditional English country kitchen is perfect for Capricorn. The addition of a few exposed oak beams would be ideal, since you revere age and love older properties.

and furry chenille. Interior lighting finds a place for table lamps with candlestick bases, and for brass and gold-coloured standard lamps. Wall-mounted lights with two arms, candle bulbs and fabric shades will also complement this scheme. Your awareness of social prestige would not even rule out the odd chandelier.

Kitchen

You are not overly concerned with food, but you do like to entertain on important family occasions and for business purposes. Your kitchen therefore needs designing for efficient functioning at all times. A range-type cooker makes the ideal centre point since, although you will resent the initial expense, you will ultimately appreciate the durability, reputation and the chance to impress your friends.

The kitchen floor should undoubtedly be tiled in stone – slate, a dark marble or granite would provide the requisite subdued colour. This theme could be continued to provide material for your kitchen's work surfaces, with splashbacks and so forth of a matching dark colour. Kitchen units should be moulded, panelled and made from a dark wood such as mahogany, walnut or aged oak. Modern kitchen appliances will look completely out of place within such a traditional environment, so should be hidden away inside purpose-built cupboards and drawers.

Finally, a ceramic butler's sink, copper saucepans and enamel kitchenware will be much more in keeping with the Capricorn style than modern aluminium and stainless steel alternatives. A brass swan-neck mixer tap provides the perfect finishing touch.

Bedroom

A classic four-poster bed perfectly suits the Capricorn connection with tradition and with the past, but would probably be considered a little ostentatious for your rather conservative tastes. An imposing mahogany *bateau lit* proves a favoured alternative, replete with its characteristically curved headboard and baseboard, and still giving the necessary appearance of quality and solidity. Such an unusual and distinctive choice would certainly form a stunning centrepiece within your bedchamber, without hinting at the affectation which might be associated with the former option.

White sheets, blankets, a bedspread and an eiderdown will then provide a more traditional bed dressing than a quilt or duvet. A large free-standing mahogany wardrobe, dark wooden chest of drawers and similar dressing table collectively offer necessary storage as well as forming complementary additions to the bedroom furniture. A circular bedside table covered with a patterned fabric is a great conclusion, while a shaded bedside light confers the necessary atmospheric ambience. Quality carpet on the floor is, of course, the only sensible decision.

Bathroom

The tiled black-and-white chequerboard floor in the entrance hall can be echoed in your bathroom, but using larger tiles that better suit the greater space available. Glazed black-and-white ceramic tiles in a diamond pattern create a really powerful impact, especially when juxtaposed with a brass or gold handset mixer for the bath, gold fittings for the sink and plain walls painted in a similar golden colour.

The bathroom walls can be covered in white ceramic tiles to dado level, both serving a practical purpose and encouraging a smooth visual transition from one decorative scheme to the next. By topping this with a border of

ABOVE Your solid and traditionally styled bed is a fitting centrepiece for the Capricorn bedroom. You may prefer sheets, blankets and an eiderdown to a quilt or duvet.

Art and ornaments

Capricorn rules both pottery and sculpture, as well as stone and wood in general. Therefore a few items of old porcelain, a bust of an important historical figure, or any kind of traditional sculpture – the older the better – would all find pride of place within your home. Brass and gilded accessories, such as mirrors or picture frames, also match the Capricorn theme. The link this sign has with the structural components of the body could also mean the odd animal hide on display, or perhaps a pair of horns hung on the wall as a trophy.

predominantly black ornate tiles, and by including a black toilet seat and bathroom furniture, the general theme will be strikingly accentuated. Sanitary ware should be plain and by contrast in white; also, if possible, it should follow a somewhat period theme. A pedestal basin, slipper bath and toilet with an old-fashioned high-level cistern would all prove excellent additions from a decorative perspective.

ABOVE The Capricorn bathroom is also reminiscent of a bygone age. Here the plain black and white décor gives an impression of quality when combined with brass taps and shower fittings.

Flowers and plants

Most Capricorn plants grow best in the harsher conditions found out of doors, although amaranthus (known as love-lies-bleeding) and certain ornamental ivies can be grown inside. The aspidistra was called the 'cast iron plant' by the Victorians, since it will thrive in the kinds of cold, dark conditions that are all too easily associated with the Capricorn environment. Otherwise, since this sign has several trees with which it is linked, how about starting a couple of bonsai specimens? The kinds of discipline and root-pruning associated with this art are surely Capricorn principles exemplified.

LEFT Dedicating a certain amount of space to your working life is advisable for Capricorn, since you'll always have plenty to do and will often bring work home.

Extra room

Bearing in mind your love of work – in particular out of hours and at home – the ideal extra room in the Capricorn household must be an office. Don't expect this to include contemporary office furniture, though. Obviously, for most jobs nowadays an administrative centre needs a certain amount of technology. This might include a telephone, fax machine, photocopier, printer, computer and so forth. Certainly, most Capricorns have adopted the phone and the photocopier and will prepare to grapple manfully with the fax machine. However, when it comes to computers there are many still clunking along with that ancient manual typewriter which looked pretty good when your grandmother was a girl.

Nevertheless, you are going to need a desk, a chair, a certain amount of storage and the space in which to work. Otherwise, the more the indications of modern life can be hidden away the happier you are. So computers housed in antique roll-top desks would be more or less perfect, with the desk drawers used for filing purposes. Mahogany or walnut bureaus containing fax machines and buttoned leather desk chairs doubling as typist stools are both also good indicators of Capricorn's style.

Combining with others

Aries

Capricorn is an earth sign and Aries is a fire sign, so ordinarily one wouldn't expect these two to get along. However, they are both such strong characters that often an atmosphere of mutual respect prevails. A Capricorn scheme of decoration predominates, although Aries will always speak up when they really don't agree.

Taurus

Since you are both earth signs, you are likely to share a similarly conservative and practical perspective on home decoration. You both value good quality, although Taurus may need to fight for the odd more luxurious item, which Capricorn will doubtless consider to be an unnecessary extravagance. Otherwise, a good match.

Gemini

Gemini and Capricorn don't make a good combination. Gemini is too drawn to variety, is too changeable and leaves too many things unfinished for Capricorn. Capricorn believes that many of Gemini's ideas are based on transient values with only superficial worth. You also feel their interests are pure frivolity.

Cancer

You both have a traditional approach to home design and in many ways your tastes and opinions are much the same. However, your own home can easily become a cold, lifeless museum. Cancer will certainly help to bring that warmer touch – with more rounded forms, softness and love. There will be plenty to eat, too.

Leo

The two of you both aim to be noticed and appreciated, so this will always help provide some common ground to share. However, your own preference is for subdued and understated quality while Leo's is much more showy, so you will probably think them a little brash and ostentatious on occasion.

Virgo

Capricorn and Virgo share a similar interest in quality, although the Virgo style is more modest and less monumental than that of Capricorn, although probably all the more user-friendly as a consequence. Virgo's style is also rather more contemporary, yet still presented in a quiet and unthreateningly earthy way.

Libra

You will probably find Libra a little frivolous in their design choices. Librans tend to place great value on beautiful appearances and on an environment conducive to social interaction. You will emphasize the practicalities to a much greater degree. You don't always see the purpose of those finer touches.

Scorpio

Scorpio can spend a lot of time precisely arranging their home environment. Generally speaking, you wouldn't have the patience for this, although you would certainly make an effort when needed, such as when preparing for important guests. Otherwise, you don't really mind, though you definitely wouldn't want to dust everything.

Sagittarius

Your approach to your home life is rigid and controlled. You like a tidy house, have high standards of behaviour and high expectations of others. Sagittarians by contrast are relaxed and carefree. Their housework is irregular and they prefer a more lived-in feel. The potential for conflict is considerable.

Other Capricorn

While you are certainly in agreement regarding a traditionally conservative approach, there could still be some potential for discord on occasions. This is most likely where the typically stark and no-frills approach of the male Capricorn proves at variance with the rather more elaborate ideas of his feminine counterpart.

Aquarius

These two signs are in many ways representatives of opposing principles. Capricorn shows permanence, tradition and a conservative approach. Aquarius augurs change, a revolutionary outcome and a departure from all that has gone before. Perhaps a large house with totally separate areas is the best solution.

Pisces

Pisces often needs a little guidance. Ideally, these compassionate and intuitive souls are best supported by a more practical yet sympathetic associate. Capricorn immediately recognizes this Piscean vulnerability and quickly assumes control. Providing they don't completely crush their creativity, everything should be fine.

Priorities: *modernity, individualism, progressiveness, unconventionality.*

The typical Aquarius

Aquarians are astrologically famous as the individualists of the zodiac. At times they can be wild, wacky, unpredictable, obstinate, awkward, eccentric and perverse. They are renowned for their progressive views, extreme outlook, disregard for convention and for their exceptional love of freedom. Nevertheless, most Aquarians are driven by the best of motivations. They will strive to be egalitarian in their perspective and won't worry unduly if some people consider their more outrageous views to be a little mad.

Aquarians will fearlessly expound unpopular beliefs with a genuine concern for the whole of humanity. Ruled by the planet Uranus, they are often gifted exponents of information technology, astrology and of other New Age concerns. Aquarians will inevitably be at the vanguard of the forthcoming Aquarian Age, easily presenting metaphysical concepts in a palatable form for others to understand. On a personal level, however, Aquarians should be careful that their classic distinguishing characteristics do not go too far. Individuality can turn easily to isolation. Cheerful eccentricity may sometimes seem a little weird.

The Aquarius home

Aquarius is the sign most associated with the paradox and with juxtaposition, where for example strangely anomalous and apparently unrelated objects are closely linked with one another to produce visually striking effects. Nowhere is this more apparent than in the Aquarian home. Here the very old and the very new, the traditional and the ultra-modern are placed side by side in a way that would normally never be considered. The effect is certainly eye-catching and in the Aquarian home, at least, it somehow seems to work.

Thus the typical Aquarian would ideally live deep in the country or right in the centre of town, but never anywhere in between. They would love a rambling rural retreat at the end of circuitous country roads, or a loft, penthouse or warehouse conversion where the city never sleeps. The main similarity is that either location requires some effort to reach and that the Aquarian will know you are coming, preferably from some distance away.

Characteristics

Favourable

Progressive • humanitarian • egalitarian • independent • unconventional • friendly • rational • fair

Less favourable

Contrary • rebellious • eccentric • perverse • self-willed • erratic • unstable • cold

Sign associations

Symbol The Water Bearer

Ruling planet Uranus

Day of the week Friday

Lucky colours Electric blue, turquoise and black

Lucky number Four

Birthstones Amethyst and opal

Metals Uranium, aluminium, maybe platinum

Flowers All orchid species

Trees Laburnum, citrus trees, most fruit trees

Regions Ethiopia, Finland, Iran, Russia, Sweden and Syria

Towns and cities Bremen, Brighton, Hamburg, Helsinki, Moscow, Salzburg and St Petersburg

Best partners Gemini and Libra

Worst partners Taurus and Scorpio

Ten key factors

built-in fixtures and equipment
computers
electricity
gadgets
light and lighting
modernization
new technology
paradoxes
stereo systems
television

built-in fixtures

gadgets

An air sign

Aquarius shares the same cerebral, rational and intellectual outlook that characterizes all the air signs. Aquarians are not renowned for their sentimental or emotional response and tend to look at matters coolly, rationally and with a degree of detachment. They are basically social, but differ in valuing independence and their own space equally greatly. Often they need time alone to pursue their own personal interests.

In terms of colour, Aquarians are traditionally linked with the blues of the air palette, but also with the addition of startling electric shades to provide a contemporary feel. Great views are also essential for their ideal home, with a generally open and airy feel.

ABOVE A modern inner city warehouse or loft conversion is perfect for Aquarius, especially with a commanding viewpoint and with no need for curtains to deter prying eyes.

light and lighting

television

modernization

Making an entrance

Ideal Aquarian homes are found in the heart of the country and right in the centre of town. The latter is the more distinctive, but both locations share a number of features. For the visitor, the former will be hard to find at the end of a lengthy drive. Since it is the only residence around, you will hear and see their car for some distance. Visitors are unlikely to venture there on the off chance, so the more determined will need to make advance arrangements with you for their reception.

The same is true of the inner-city loft conversion, in many ways the more typically Aquarian option. It is also inaccessible, since inner-city traffic and parking restrictions will again tend to discourage the casual passer-by. It is well protected both in terms of its lofty location and the entryphones, alarms and buzzer systems that its location demands. Again, you receive plentiful warning of any visitor's approach.

Living areas

Assuming the inner-city warehouse conversion to represent your perfect home, the first noticeable thing once comfortably inside is its open-plan nature and the immediate impression of unrestricted space. This is very important to the average Aquarian, who belongs to the air element and benefits enormously from having a great deal of it around. The next thing to catch attention are the huge undressed windows and staggering views, stretching way out over the surrounding city and further increasing the feeling of unlimited space and freedom.

Plain varnished floorboards are perhaps the perfect choice of flooring for your loft, with the walls in most instances left as bare brick. An alternative is plain white emulsion, with one wall highlighted as a bright, strong statement to act as a focal point. Your furniture is ultra-modern and forms an interesting contrast with the fairly basic surrounds. There is an enormous black leather and chrome designer sofa with matching armchairs, plus a minimalist chrome and glass coffee table and a large strikingly patterned geometric rug on the floor. Finally, there is a huge wide-screen plasma television and the latest home-entertainment system, all packaged together in brushed metal finish.

Flooring

Sanded and varnished wooden floorboards are an easy choice for the Aquarian home. White painted floorboards can look great, too. Some of the newer resin and rubber floors are an excellent contemporary selection, particular those with more outrageous finishes, or which mimic older materials and thus emphasize your propensity for mixing the old and new. Finally, there is always metal flooring for those who would favour a really industrial result.

Lighting

Again, the most modern technologies are best suited to Aquarius, so the latest in ceiling recessed halogen spotlights and indeed any kind of unusual

ABOVE Whether in the heart of the country or in the centre of town you're unlikely to be passing the ideal Aquarian residence, which may prove quite difficult to reach.

Fabrics and wallpaper

Ideal fabrics for your home are those that make bold statements and which counteract the plain and somewhat austere nature of their surroundings. Striking animal prints are especially recommended – for example fake leopard skin, zebra or cowhide. Although you would never support the slaughter of wild animals purely for decorative purposes, you are more able to justify the use of real leather and suede.

lighting design will be perfect for you. Otherwise, natural daylight should be maximized with huge windows, great views and no curtains at all, wherever possible. Where necessary, window treatments must be streamlined and stylized. Plain metal Venetian blinds, wooden shutters and basic cotton roller-blinds would all ideally suit you.

ABOVE Aquarius loves new inventions, techniques and ideas. The use of sheet metal panelling for this breakfast bar is certainly innovative and helps to create the ultra-modern atmosphere you adore.

Kitchen

The nature of your open-plan abode is such that the kitchen area may be only separated by means of the intelligent arrangement of furniture into clearly demarcated zones, or through the clever use of room dividers such as open-sided shelves. A gleaming stainless steel range is its primary feature, with a matching splashback and integral steel extractor hood, all highlighted beautifully by the halogen spotlights that track across the ceiling here.

Since the urban Aquarian is likely to eat out a lot and will probably exist on takeaways and snacks meanwhile, the ultra-modern theme of your kitchen can really be accentuated without the need to be overly concerned with daily practicalities. Thus there is also the potential for steel, zinc or titanium tiles to be used on walls and surfaces, or even as textured variations on the floor for a truly continuous look.

Alternatively, a mixture of fitted and free-standing kitchen units is preferable for such an open arrangement, mainly finished in white or a pale wood which complements the dominantly metallic theme. Glass and chrome fittings also find their place, together with wall-hung racks of steel cooking utensils and an oversized fridge in a bulbous retro design.

ABOVE This urban bedroom is kept free from clutter by the generous provision of floor-to-ceiling cupboard space, made even less obtrusive by its mirrored façade.

Bedroom

Within such a modernist urban environment, your bedroom is likely to prove minimalist in its approach. Consequently, excellent storage is essential, in order to remove life's everyday clutter from obvious display. Fitted floor-to-ceiling cupboards would be perfect for such a scheme, with perhaps a mirrored-glass façade disguising their presence and to maximize the impression of light and space. Similarly, a large shelving unit consisting of entirely open cubes would hold a wide selection of bits and pieces, while complementing rather than detracting from the intentionally stark and contemporary impression.

The bed should be modern, but with some unusual touches to reflect your quirkiness. It could be wooden and low to the floor, or made of plain metal with a brushed metallic surface and enhanced with scaffolding poles. Sleeping on a raised platform high above your surroundings would also suit Aquarius. Brick for the walls might prove a little too industrial, so plain white emulsion is probably the best alternative. One whole wall could then be painted in a totally contrasting hue.

Bathroom

Remembering the Aquarian association with everything modern and progressive, certain more recent design trends can usefully be highlighted within your bathroom. The technology behind the production of interior design materials has advanced enormously. For example, it is now possible to

Art and ornaments

Decoration is probably best kept fairly sparse in the Aquarian home, in order to avoid any feeling of clutter. Unusual large-scale modern art is great as a focal point, as would be some atypically shaped ornaments and vases, or a few simple ceramics arranged within the groups that Aquarius rules. A couple of very old or unusual items, such as a rare African carving, a piece of crystal or an ancient item of Neolithic art, would also serve to highlight the paradoxes with which you are closely linked.

purchase resin flooring in a pearlescent finish, the colour of which changes according to the viewing angle and surrounding lighting. Such a spectacular and futuristic effect would surely be perfect for you – it would definitely complement the whole tenor of your ideal home.

Otherwise, transparent is a great theme to follow, since if transparent were a colour it would certainly belong to this sign. Glass bricks could find application for dividing off the shower cubicle. A transparent sink is a great touch, either in clear or frosted glass and with a burnished or metallic finish for a truly stunning first impression. A modern ergonomically designed and free-standing bath, with either a brushed aluminium or steel surround, would continue the cutting-edge scenario, as would halogen spotlights recessed into the ceiling and mosaic tiles lining the whole walls. These tiles could echo the metallic theme too.

ABOVE The Aquarian bathroom is also minimalist in its approach and features the latest design trends and materials. You'll probably prefer showers to baths, on account of your busy lifestyle.

Flowers and plants

Orchids are especially associated with Aquarius and there are many different kinds from which to choose. From moth orchids to tiger and slipper orchids, there are now many varieties available for indoor cultivation, some of which will with a little care stay in flower nearly all year round. Besides, the stunning beauty of any orchid flower will easily reward the effort spent. Not so long ago these plants were only for experts; nowadays they are found tumbling from the pages of any design magazine.

LEFT The Internet is a typically Aquarian medium, since although you can be friendly with everyone, nobody gets really close. Aquarians have an affinity with all kinds of computer technology.

Extra room

You love any kind of gadgetry. You belong to the sign most closely associated with new ideas, modern technology and computers. Generally speaking, Aquarians always were gifted with such things, but the advent of the Internet certainly has moved matters up a level. Now, instead of tinkering in solitude with a single isolated machine, Aquarians are simultaneously able to make and to maintain friends from all over the world. You can communicate in real time with people from exotic and far-flung locations and relate with an informality which previously would have taken years to achieve. At the same time you can maintain the physical distance which only e-mail permits. So the ideal Aquarian extra room would be somewhere to use your computer equipment.

There should be at least one state-of-the-art computer system, together with a flat-panel monitor and up-to-the-minute colour printer. Some serious speakers and a scanner would also go down well. In the background, the latest stereo system in a brushed-metal design provides additional entertainment. A basic modern desk in a pale wood such as pine, an angled desk lamp and a suitable chair for typing largely serve to complete this high-tech picture.

Combining with others

Aries

Aquarius is orientated towards the future and is always well ahead where the latest design trends are concerned. Aries views themselves as a leader and an initiator, so will appreciate the insider knowledge of Aquarius in enabling them to be among the first to adopt new ideas.

Taurus

Taurean tastes are far too predictable for Aquarius. Their focus on tradition fails to excite your interest and their obsession with comfort proves uninspiring. Although you can certainly appreciate the Taurean's natural aesthetic flair, you would much rather experiment with strange new materials and with cutting-edge design.

Gemini

Aquarius is certainly revolutionary, but you can sometimes become a little stuck in your own ways of thinking and in established modes of creative expression. Gemini has read all the latest magazines and can talk extensively of the hottest trends. Aquarius can't help but be fascinated by such stimulating input.

Cancer

Aquarius and Cancer probably don't have a great deal in common, since Cancer has a very traditional view of their home environment and Aquarius is forever breaking the mould. However, many Aquarians value their own space highly, so perhaps in this respect you'll build a safe and secure home together.

Leo

These signs are actually similar, since they both have their own ways of doing things and are both very certain that these are right. Putting them together can't be recommended, since under normal circumstances they will both want their own way totally. The spirit of compromise can be very scarce indeed.

Virgo

Although you admire the simplistic and natural approach to interior design that Virgo personifies, your own approach is rather more eclectic. You find it hard to stick rigidly to any kind of decorative scheme, so will tend to mess up Virgo's carefully laid plans with your own unexpected and individual additions.

Libra

Aquarius and Libra are both air signs, so the potential for a happy relationship is certainly there. At times, you may feel that the harmonious and easy-going Libran approach is getting a little too comfortable, so you will then try to stir things up with your own astonishing input.

Scorpio

It is not recommended for you to live together, since you both have your own sets of ideas and are unlikely to take interference. Scorpio is the more fixed of the two, so a broadly Scorpio theme with the odd Aquarian touch would really represent the only compromise. This probably won't last, however.

Sagittarius

Sagittarius and Aquarius are quite similar. You both need a lot of space within your domestic environment, both enjoy decorative elements from other cultures and both value your independence highly. Aquarius has a much more modernist and futuristic approach, but you should still agree on most things.

Capricorn

Ask Aquarius about their worst nightmare and to personify the design traits against which they are trying to rebel. The answer really would be typified by the average Capricorn home. The mannered approach, extreme reverence for tradition, the strict and stuffy atmosphere. There is not much scope for consensus here.

Other Aquarius

Put two Aquarians together and the result will certainly be very startling and futuristic. It might also prove rather uncomfortable, cold and stark. Although the latest design materials are undoubtedly pretty amazing, they often weren't used beforehand for a very good reason. Aluminium space blankets, anyone?

Pisces

Aquarius likes their residence to be spacious and uncluttered, whereas Pisces would feel totally exposed in such an environment. Pisces likes lots of items to hide behind, whereas Aquarius would soon feel frustrated by constantly banging into things. Consequently, Aquarius and Pisces don't really mix that well.

Priorities: *seclusion, kindness, creativity, music, intuition, faith.*

The typical Pisces

Many zodiac signs are described as sensitive, but Pisces is truly the most sensitive of all. Those born under its influence are gentle, receptive, intuitive, compassionate, charitable, and are often spiritually orientated. They can be poetic, artistic and musical, but are easily hurt and confused by the harsher realities of a daily existence. Typically, Pisceans would sit up all night listening to a friend's problems. However, tidiness, practicality and paying their bills on time can present rather more of a challenge.

Otherwise Pisceans are probably best described as nebulous. They tend to adopt differing personas depending on present company. They may fall prey to escapism and sometimes to the abuse of drugs and alcohol. They can also be gullible and susceptible to the influence of stronger individuals.

Nevertheless, under perfect circumstances the Piscean principle represents an ideal to which everyone should aspire. When the importance of another's welfare equals that of the self, the main teachings of many of the world's main religions become embodied in reality.

The Pisces home

Pisceans tend to fall into two camps where their home life is concerned. Typically, Pisces is not a tidy sign, being literally associated with chaos, a rulership which may easily become all too apparent. Those born under this sign are often not characterized by effective organization or by an ordered and structured approach to everyday affairs. They are ethereal creatures, whose existence encompasses much more of the otherworldly and the intuitive, rather than focusing on the dull practicalities of the everyday.

In practice, therefore, it can be surprising just how many Pisceans react against these often-mentioned tendencies to live in homes that are very effectively organized indeed. This apparently contradictory expression serves to pinpoint the duality associated with this sign and can incline its subjects towards an almost fanatical emphasis on efficiency and order. When it could prove all too easy to drift away into a sea of endless possibilities, a tidy home provides the essential anchor for keeping your feet on the ground.

Characteristics

Favourable

Compassionate • caring • charitable • receptive • idealistic • psychic • imaginative • unassuming

Less favourable

Impractical • vague • helpless • confused • unreliable • escapist • disorganized • manipulative

Sign associations

Symbol The Fishes

Ruling planet Neptune

Day of the week Thursday and Friday

Lucky colours Sea green, aquamarine, lilac and mauve

Lucky number Seven, perhaps three

Birthstones Aquamarine, emerald and coral

Metals Platinum, tin and zinc

Flowers Moss, seaweed, water lilies and other aquatic plants

Trees Fig, willow, trees growing in or near water

Regions Egypt, Normandy, North Africa, Portugal, Samoa and Scandinavia

Towns and cities Alexandria, Bournemouth, Cowes, Grimsby, Jerusalem, Seville and Warsaw

Best partners Cancer, Scorpio, Leo and Aquarius

Worst partners Gemini, Sagittarius, Virgo

Ten key factors

aquariums
fountains
mazes
oil
sand
sea
secrets
veils
water
wells

aquariums

mazes

A water sign

Pisces is the third of the water signs. The associations of these signs with water can be categorized as follows. Cancer is the ruler of lakes, streams and rivers. Scorpio rules ponds, pools and marshy areas. Pisces rules the vast depths and expanses most often found within the ocean and the sea.

A watery theme is therefore ideal for the Piscean home. This can be emphasized through the use of water features both inside and outside, or by having a colourful aquarium placed in a prominent location. Likewise, by using natural materials and a little imagination, a beachcomber theme can be continued throughout the home.

ABOVE The living areas of the Pisces home may seem untidy or even a little chaotic, but the atmosphere is always warm and welcoming. A minimalist approach doesn't suit your sign.

sea

veils

fountains

Making an entrance

On first approach, your home may not appear particularly imposing. This sign is often rather humble and self-effacing. Over the years, you will gradually learn that some degree of a material focus is important, since monetary resources equal choice, space and the freedom to decide for yourself. However, living life according to your own spiritual and emotional ideals is actually the most important factor, rather than any great desire to impress or to draw attention to your achievements.

Pisceans also greatly value seclusion and privacy, so would not wish to be noticed unduly by the outside world. So you may live down a quiet backstreet or in a nondescript suburban area, where your true identity is hidden behind the anonymity of your surroundings. Ideally, though, you would definitely like to live close to the sea. Meanwhile, the first thing the visitor will notice upon entering your abode is the number of shoes in the hallway. Pisceans always seem to suffer with their feet.

Living areas

Your home is essentially a haven from the stresses of the outside world. Therefore the living areas should be as cosy and restful as possible. Should you live in a busy area, double glazing is essential, helping you to find the peace you crave. Your heating system should be more than adequate, with gas and oil both ruled by your sign. Although you would love an open fire, you are probably better off with quicker and easier modern alternatives.

Privacy is also a major factor, so yours is a sign that prefers the windows to be covered, unless you live surrounded by greenery or have a great view over the sea. Good light is important to you, so loose drapes of a lightweight or sheer material will effectively exclude the outside world, while still permitting the daylight free passage. Informally dressing your windows with chiffon, muslin, gauze, organza or voile in a sunlight colour will serve effectively to brighten even the darkest of days.

Aquamarine, azure, sky blue and turquoise make for a great complementary colour scheme, contrasting with distressed white painted furniture and floorboards for a real beachside feel.

Flooring

Sanded floorboards are the best option throughout your home. These can be left plain, whitewashed with a resilient white emulsion, or bleached, limed or given a more subtle semi-opaque finish by treating with white paint mixed into a clear varnish. Natural flooring such as seagrass or sisal is also eminently suitable, with natural toned and textured carpets for extra comfort.

Lighting

Pisceans are not fond of bright or direct light, so lighting within your perfect home should ideally be natural, indirect, gentle and diffuse. Candlelight is a

ABOVE The entrance to the Piscean home may have little to make it stand out, since yours is a sign which values seclusion and that is often modest in the extreme.

Fabrics and wallpaper

Wallpaper doesn't find too great an application within the Piscean home. An ideal wall covering for you would be wooden tongue-and-groove boarding. This could be used to dado height in hallways, to emphasize a focal wall in your bedroom or almost everywhere within the bathroom and the kitchen. Otherwise, the best Piscean fabrics are floaty, semi-transparent and ethereal.

great favourite in many different situations and low-level lighting from stylish table lamps is much to be preferred over the harsher overhead variety. Clear glass lanterns finished in brushed metal or plain white enamel can also prove an interesting feature.

ABOVE Pisces is one sign that doesn't mind a small kitchen, since you'll be more easily able to keep your culinary exploits under control and to reach whatever you need.

Kitchen

Pisces is one sign for whom a small kitchen works well. It will be easy to keep everything clean and under control, and you will be able to reach from the cooker to the sink and back to the cupboard, ensuring that all your culinary exploits reach a successful and aptly timed conclusion. A narrow galley kitchen also fits perfectly with the maritime theme.

It is a good idea to keep matters simple, maintaining a relaxed decorative theme within the kitchen. Fitted units are best in a confined space. These could be finished in a straightforward tongue-and-groove or in a Shaker-derived style. A light wood such as pine would be appropriate, or there is distressed white or one of the range of blues used previously. Glossy and overly reflective surfaces are not recommended within this natural and informal setting.

The original floorboards would probably be best underfoot – once more painted, limed or otherwise distressed to emphasize the cheerful, relaxed, almost holiday atmosphere. Then there are chequered blue and white café curtains on the windows and a matching cotton rug for the floor. An additional selection of open storage options houses your cutlery, crockery and assorted kitchen utensils.

Bedroom

The perfect Piscean bedroom serves to continue the distressed and limewashed theme. Imagine an atmosphere reminiscent of seaside holidays, of hot lazy beachside days and of driftwood naturally aged through prolonged contact with water and the sun. Sisal or seagrass flooring is perfect for initially evoking an atmosphere reminiscent of a beach hut, especially when combined with whitewash or semi-transparent colour on the walls and floors, quite possibly with tongue-and-groove panelling for the walls too. The harsher texture of natural flooring can be minimized by using blue or white textured cotton rugs in sensitive locations. A texture-weave carpet in a natural tone could be a softer though less authentic alternative.

Additional bedroom furniture should be mismatched and similarly distressed, possibly gathered over time from junk shops, house clearances and from car-boot sales. A wardrobe, chest of drawers and an old wooden chair would all be perfect. Ideally, these items should also be in bleached wooden shades or in a distressed white. A white-painted wrought-iron or naturally coloured pine bed then acts as a centrepiece. Plain linen or cotton Roman blinds are a simple complementary touch for windows.

Bathroom

Obviously, it is in your bathroom that the theme of oceans and the sea can find its most flamboyant expression. It is better to keep the backdrop fairly simple, since it is the minor features that will be most emphasized here. A plain wooden floor with off-white walls, tongue-and-groove panelling to dado level, a simple roller-blind and mismatched furniture painted in a distressed white all help to set the backdrop for these all-important finishing touches. A round bathroom mirror reminiscent of a porthole would be an interesting addition.

Art and ornaments

Ornamentation should largely serve to emphasize the watery, marine and maritime themes found elsewhere in your home. Seashells such as abalone, mother-of-pearl decorations, dried starfish, sea urchins and coral are all excellent additions. Simple pebbles can also be used to amazing effect, particularly when grouped together in interesting or unexpected locations. Paintings or photographs featuring the ocean would be a good idea too.

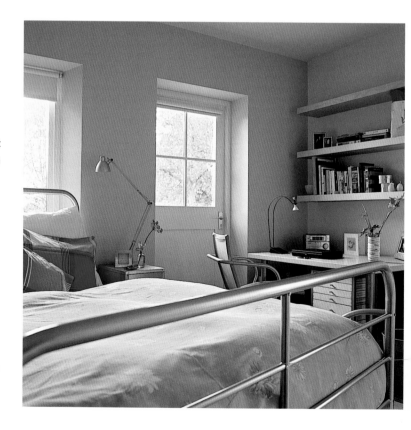

BELOW A soothing atmosphere is promoted by the use of pastel colours and translucent white cotton blinds. It's unlikely the Piscean bedroom would stay this tidy for long, however.

Blue walls and window shutters would suit equally well, as would painted tongue-and-groove panelling around the bath. Look for a free-standing roll-top bath, and complete the marine theme with dried starfish, seashells, pebbles, coral, sponges, cuttlefish bones and driftwood. These items can be tastefully arranged around the room for maximum impact. Pebbles can even be used to form unusual door handles and hanging light switches for the more creatively inclined. Finally, sea-scented candles will generate the romantic ambience that you so love.

ABOVE Pisces is linked with the ocean. The bathroom is an especially important room in your home and is a wonderful environment in which to expand upon this maritime theme.

Extra room

Pisceans love water. You love relaxing in a luxuriously deep bath, but really enjoy the opportunity to immerse yourself more fully. Therefore the ideal extra room in the Piscean home would house your own swimming pool. Obviously, this is entering the realms of fantasy where many properties are concerned. Less costly alternatives might include an indoor or outdoor jacuzzi or even a hot tub, both places where Pisces could bathe away the worries and the cares of the day. In warmer locations, an inflatable pool is certainly better than nothing, although far from ideal.

Pisceans love the natural world, but aren't particularly hardy. A heated outdoor pool covered by a glass dome would suit you best, with the potential for this covering to be removed when the weather permits. The glass cover would enable you to see through and to appreciate nature's beauty, while being protected from the worst vagaries of the external environment. A blue or golden tint to the pool's cover would be perfect because, as with using coloured semi-transparent window treatments indoors, a sunshine tint often serves to brighten even the darkest days.

ABOVE A swimming pool would certainly be the perfect addition to any Piscean home. As a sign you're not hardy, so a heated or covered pool is best in temperate climes.

Flowers and plants

Aquatic plants are ruled by Pisces and there usually isn't much scope for their cultivation within the average home. Therefore some suitably coloured glass or ceramic vases filled with dried reeds, rushes or a few plants drawn from coastal locations would certainly echo the appropriate themes. As an alternative, a few large leafy plants from the rainforest might prove to be an acceptable substitute.

Combining with others

Aries
An Aries expression is far too blunt and insensitive for poor Pisces, who would soon feel like a fish out of water in this brutal design environment. There is little middle ground between these two decorative schemes, so only with extreme awareness from Aries could any compromise be reached.

Taurus
Pisces and Taurus have a fair amount in common and so could probably live together rather well. Taurus could concentrate on the larger elements of the home environment – a luxurious sofa for example – and then Pisces could enter with dreamlike additions once the main structural elements are in place.

Gemini
Gemini likes lots of interesting additions to their decorative scheme, but not really in the same way that Pisces does. Gemini thinks of the Piscean's lifestyle as disorganized and chaotic; Pisces feels that Gemini is lacking in warmth. The difference is subtle but obvious to members of the signs concerned.

Cancer
Cancer is a nurturing and sympathetic character who will take pleasure in encouraging Pisces to develop their own creative impulses. Cancer is not the type to make others feel small or to hinder their personal development, and they will always do their utmost to provide a safe and secure base.

Leo
Leo is a fire sign and Pisces is water, so there would not usually be a harmonious relationship between the two. However, uniquely Pisces feels attracted to and warmed by Leo's strength of personality, and will always be ready to admire unswervingly some of their more outrageous design exploits.

Virgo
Virgo is too pedantic for Pisces, too analytical, tidy and critical. Pisces may not be the greatest at practicalities, but in terms of compassion, imagination and creative ability you are one of the best. You really don't need somebody telling you that you are wrong all the time. This is not a good match.

Libra
You don't really feel either way. You are both quite indecisive, so put together you have the potential to disappear in a haze of confusion. You respect one another's design choices, but somehow find it hard to get inspired. There are no huge problems, either, but can indifference constitute a recommendation?

Scorpio
Scorpio is very strong-willed and, since you are so malleable, you will only receive whatever creative opportunities the Scorpion is happy to allow. Still, there is some affinity since you are both water signs. Providing you can still express yourself somehow, at least you will always appreciate knowing where you stand.

Sagittarius
There is not a lot of love here. Sagittarius is too blunt and clumsy and you really have very different lifestyles and expectations from your home. You know that they don't mean any harm but, once your delicate decorative constructions have been flattened a few times, you will probably be ready to pack your bags.

Capricorn
Pisceans are drawn to Capricorns, since they are attracted by the air of calm capability that accompanies this sign. However, the Capricorn decorative style is really too strict and formal for such an impressionable and acquiescent sign, with Pisces maybe missing out on opportunities to express your talents fully.

Aquarius
You often feel that Aquarius understands your language, at least a great deal better than many other signs. However, when it comes to décor and design, there is rather more of a gap between you. Aquarian lines are modern and clear-cut; yours are much more sentimental and diffuse.

Other Pisces
You will definitely be able to make the perfect water-themed home. You could also create a fantasy land where you can disappear together and never be seen again. Often in such a situation one Piscean gradually becomes extremely practical, probably to avoid this couple losing contact with reality completely.

Index

Acknowledgements

Executive Editor Sarah Tomley
Senior Editor Rachel Lawrence
Executive Art Editor Leigh Jones
Designer Colin Goody
Production Controller Ian Paton
Picture Researcher Luzia Strohmayer

Picture Acknowledgements

Abode 5 centre, 16 right, 25 bottom, 32, 54, 56, 58, 72, 74, 79, 86, 113, 120, 121
Alamy/Alan Weintraub 106
Arcaid/David Churchill 42 /David Churchill/ architect: Your Home 114 /Nicholas Kane/ architect: Robert Sakula & Cany Ash 47 /Simon Kenny/ stylist: Nadine Bush 117 Top /Simon Kenny/BELLE 119 /Richard Powers 37 Top /Richard Waite/ architect: Eva Jiricna 23 Bottom, 112 /Richard Waite/ architect: Moutard Architects 33
Corbis UK Ltd/Dean Conger 19 bottom /Jim Erickson 2, 21 bottom /Otto Rogge 2 top, 8–9, 13 /Bo Zaunders 90
Corbis UK Ltd. 14
Deidi von Schaewen 61 Top
Elizabeth Whiting Associates 30, 34
Fired Earth Interiors/www.firedearth.com (stockists tel: ++44 (0) 1295 814300) 37 bottom centre, 93 bottom left, 94, 100 left, 100 right, 101 bottom left, 116 left
Getty Images/Steve Dunwell 62 /Rob Melnychuk 109 bottom centre /Chris Windsor 116 right /Mel Yates 5 top, 12
Getty Images/Digital Vision 7
Graham & Brown Limited/www.grahambrown.com (stockists tel: ++44 (0) 800 3288452) 111
Homebase 60 left
The Interior Archive/Tim Beddow/ designer: De Taillac 45 top /Mark Luscombe-Whyte 85 Top /Edina van der Wyck/ architect: Richard Rogers 48
Leigh Jones 23 Top
Ray Main/ Mainstream 64, 78, 82, 89, 122 /design: John Minshaw front cover right /design: Matt Livesy Hammond front cover centre
The Mosaic Company/www.mosaiccompany.co.uk (stockists tel: ++44 (0) 1480 474714) 101 bottom right
Narratives/Jan Baldwin 39, 40, 53 Top, 55, 57, 69 Top, 71, 93 top, 97, 103, 104, 105 /Tamsyn Hill 17 left, 70 /Ashley Judge 41 /Dennis Mortell 100 top /Polly Wreford 16 left
Octopus Publishing Group Limited 93 bottom right /Mark Bolton/ design: Sarah Sanderson, RHS Chelsea 2001 53 bottom left /Steve Gorton 61 bottom left /Sebastian Hedgecoe 36 right, 49, 73, 77 top, 80 /Rupert Horrox 61 bottom centre, 92 right /Dave Jordan 36 bottom left /Sandra Lane 69 bottom centre /Di Lewis 52 left /David Loftus 29 bottom left /Tom Mannion front cover left, 29 bottom right, 37 bottom right, 44 left, 45 bottom left, 85 bottom centre, 92 left, 109 top, 109 bottom right, 109 bottom left /Mark Bolton/ design: Stephen C Markham, RHS Chelsea 2001 53 bottom centre /Peter Myers 50, 77 bottom left, 87, 108 right /David Parmitter 60 right /Peter Pugh-Cook 53 bottom right /William Reavell 44 right, 45 bottom right, 76 left, 77 bottom centre, 84 left, 84 right, 85 bottom right /Paul Ryan 85 bottom left /Mark Winwood 15 right, 52 right, 77 bottom right, 93 bottom centre, 117 bottom right /Steve Wooster 69 bottom left /Polly Wreford 28 left, 31, 45 bottom centre, 61 bottom right, 88 /Mel Yates 68 left, 68 right, 117 centre /Dominic Blackmore 29 top, 63, 95 /Neil Mersh 17 right, 96
Original Style Ltd/www. originalstyle.com (stockists tel: ++44 (0) 1392 474058) 117 bottom left, 65, 29 bottom centre, 46, 102
Papa Architects Ltd/www.papaarchitects.co.uk (tel: ++44 (0) 1392 474058) 108 left
Photodisc/Getty Images 69 bottom right
Photolibrary.com 6 /Jennifer Cheung 118 /Le Studio 38 /Watson Smith 110
Red Cover/Tim Evan-Cook 98 /Mark York 66
Reed Harris/www.reedharris.co.uk (stockists tel: ++44 (0) 20 77367511) 81, 101 bottom centre
Rubberball Productions 11, 18–19, 20–21, 24–25
Stoddard/www.stoddardcarpets.com (stockist tel: ++44 (0) 800 0724888) represented by the Carpet Foundation/ www.comebacktocarpet.com 76 right, 37 bottom left
Tiles UK Ltd./www.tilesuk.com (stockists tel: ++44 (0) 161 8725155) 28 right